The Rise & Fall of Nottingham's Railway Network

Volume 3

Off the Beaten Track

Hayden J Reed

To Alex & Robert for
accepting Daddy's trains
as something normal

Contents

Introduction

This book is a sequel to the original two volumes that charted the history of Nottingham's railways. The earlier books concentrated on public railways, and those owned or operated by the principal railway companies. These works were the realisation of an idea that had taken root more than two decades previously. Once completed however, it was apparent that they did not quite tell the full story of railways in Nottingham. Reasons of space and structure meant that some obscure, and arguably some significant subject areas could only be briefly referred to, or were left out completely. This third volume is an attempt to complete the picture and widen the study to all rail transport in Nottingham, irrespective of ownership, purpose or gauge width.

Away from the public gaze lay a railway network that has largely gone unwritten about, and which included some very interesting working arrangements. Nottingham once boasted a range of industries including mineral extraction, manufacturing and energy production. Much of this industry was rail served, and private sidings, or in some cases, complete private networks with their own locomotive fleets grew to satisfy the demand for transport of materials and goods. The decline of this hidden network has been even more dramatic than that of the public railway, and virtually none of the industrial lines looked at in this volume exist any more.

In contrast, new forms of rail use have grown up in and around the City, and again little has been written about these. The most obvious example is the return to Nottingham of trams, with the NET light rail system, opening to the public in 2004 and providing the City with a mass transit system for the 21st Century. A second and more retrospective development is the creation of the Nottingham Transport Heritage Centre, and the reopening of a portion of the Great Central's London Extension, south from Ruddington. Both of these exciting developments look to the future from very different perspectives, and each are in their own way fuelling the imagination of a fresh generation of transport enthusiasts.

In common with the two earlier books, this work does not aim at being a comprehensive technical work, or indeed a mere collection of pictures. It seeks to strike a balance between the two styles of presentation. Volume Three looks at a selection of Nottingham's industrial lines. It also explores railway preservation in the area, and takes a look at some special workings through the City and its surrounds over the years. It also returns to explore some of the hidden relics of the railway age beneath Nottingham's streets. Finally it considers the engineering aspects that went into building NET, hopefully without getting too bogged down in technical detail on the way.

The author's working career for the Highway Authority has brought him into contact with numerous projects connected with former or active railways. The largest single project he has worked on to date is undoubtedly the construction of NET. From early days of feasibility studies and outline designs, through to checking the final detail design of the tracks and ensuring they were built to Highway Authority requirements, the author spent more than a decade on the project. This has placed him in a virtually unique position to provide a technical insight into this modern success story.

Many of the photographs in this work were taken by the author, but where access to other photographers material has been kindly granted, this has been credited as appropriate. The majority of material in this volume has not been published before, excepting a handful of photographs that appeared in the earlier volumes, where these have particular relevance to the narrative and no alternatives have been available. All network maps and diagrams are copyrighted to the author.

Hayden J Reed, March 2009.

Right : Industrial steam at work in Nottinghamshire in the Sixties. The Kingston on Soar gypsum branch operated Peckett Saddle Tank 'Lady Angela' until 1970.

Photo Rob Hancock

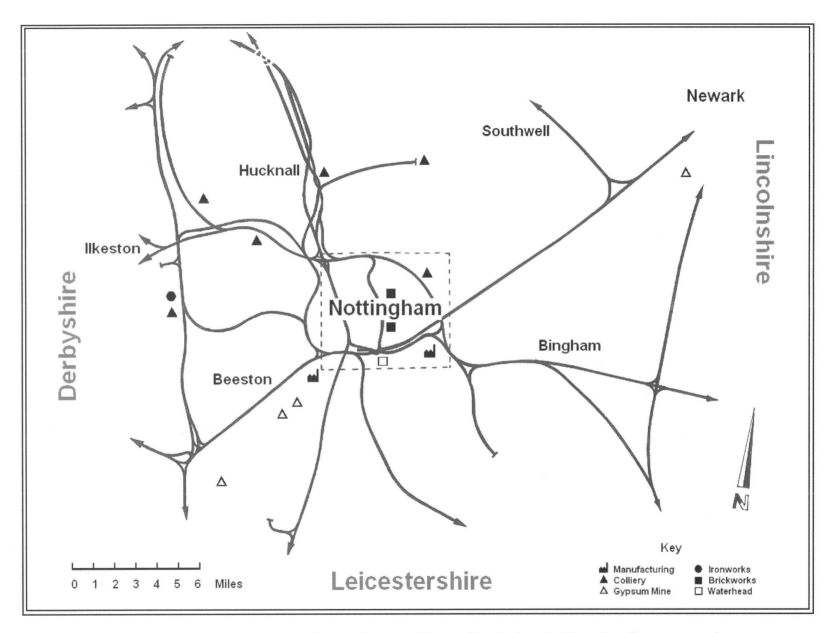

Locations of sites explored in this work, overlaid onto Nottingham's historic railway network.

The base plan above shows the area covered in the author's previous look at the public railway network around Nottingham. This volume looks at areas of rail interest associated with the City that were not covered in the first two volumes. Particular attention is paid to industrial railways, and some of the sites that are included in this work are noted on the plan above.

1.0 Tramways & Private Sidings

Coal, Gypsum, Clay, Coke, Drugs and Sewage

Public railways have always attracted a great deal of interest, but relatively little is recorded about the multitude of light railways, tramways and private sidings that served industry before the coming of motor transport. Most industrial lines were hidden away behind walls or fences, well away from the public gaze. Consequently few records of them survive.

Probably the most prolific user of private rail systems was the mineral extraction industry. This encompassed coal, clay, gravel and gypsum extraction. In the case of the collieries, extended routes connected pits and fed the main lines, whilst the sites themselves supported mazes of internal lines and sidings. With gravel and clay extraction, lightly built tramways were constructed, removed and rebuilt repeatedly to suit the changing demands of the extraction process.

Gypsum extraction in the south of the county spawned several narrow gauge lines, in addition to the better known standard gauge branches to Gotham (see Vol 2) and Kingston on Soar.

A Peckett Saddle Tank crosses Kegworth Road, en route from New Kingston Quarry in 1960. The Midland Main Line can be seen on the embankment in the background. There were once numerous private branches feeding quarries and mines across the County, Today they have all gone.

Rob Hancock

Other industries also built their own rail systems, ranging from gasworks and breweries, to manufacturers of goods and consumables. Even the ultimate end product industry, sewage processing found a use for railways.

This chapter makes no claim to be a comprehensive study (indeed Nottingham's colliery railways alone could easily fill the entire volume). What it aims to do is capture something of the diversity of private rail use that existed in and around Nottingham for a century or more before the advent of the internal combustion engine.

1.1 When Coal was King

Mining was once the predominant industry in Nottinghamshire, and the County supported many colliery railways. Railways built or operated by principal railway companies are considered in Volumes 1 and 2, but there were other notable sites and systems that operated outside the ownership of the big companies. The earliest recorded railway anywhere in England was at Wollaton, and dated from the early Seventeenth Century. This horse operated line was built for the conveyance of coal from Huntingdon Beaumont's pits at Strelley Village to Sir Percival Willoughby's Wollaton Estate. Here it would have been transferred to shallow draught barges, and moved by watercourse to the River Trent. It was probably constructed with wooden rails, along which simple tub wagons would be drawn. No remains of this exist, and even the exact route it took has been lost in time.

Mineral Lines Around Cinderhill

Nearby Cinderhill was once the focus of another privately owned, although much more recent standard gauge network that connected a string of collieries with the Nottingham Canal. The key elements dated from the early 1840s, and were constructed when local 'Coal Baron' Thomas North sank his first deep shaft at Cinderhill. Mining in the area had previously been limited to shallow 'bell pits' and small scale open workings served by lightly built tramways. Initially all of the coal from the new deep mine was dispatched via a four mile route from Cinderhill, across the present A610, and south to Babbington Wharf on the Nottingham Canal, on the southern side of Wollaton Road. The line also served Newcastle Colliery at Whitemoor, close to Nuthall Road, and crossed the Midland Railway's Trowell line on the level, with a north-west connection to the main line that today is lost beneath the embankment carrying the Ring Road (Western Boulevard).

In 1849 and 1875 respectively, direct connections were built to the Midland Railway's Leen Valley line, and to the Great Northern Derbyshire Extension. The railways quickly superseded the canal network as the main form of dispatch, and the private line took on a different role, feeding coal from Newcastle Colliery back towards a connection with the Midland Railway's complex of sidings at Radford.

Newcastle Colliery ceased production in the late 1950s, but the branch served the remaining landsale wharf at Whitemoor for another decade, after which the last of Thomas North's lines was abandoned. There were several quite substantial bridges on the route, dating from the early 1930s. These included plate steel girder bridges over Stockhill Lane and Nuthall Road. Many of these structures were built when the roads concerned were upgraded by the Highway Authority in conjunction with major new housing developments in the area. They had neatly finished blue brick abutments, and a pair of these can still be seen on Stockhill Lane.

The second main element to Thomas North's network ran due west towards collieries at Broxtowe and Kimberley. It eventually reached the Midland Railway's Erewash Valley line at Ilkeston Junction. This again ceased to be a through route prior to the Second World War.

The line was operated by an assorted collection of six-coupled saddle and side tanks in its later years, and after abandonment of the Nottingham Canal, it served landsale wharves for road distribution.

Today, few traces remain of either route, and much of the alignment has been reclaimed for development, or incorporated into private gardens.

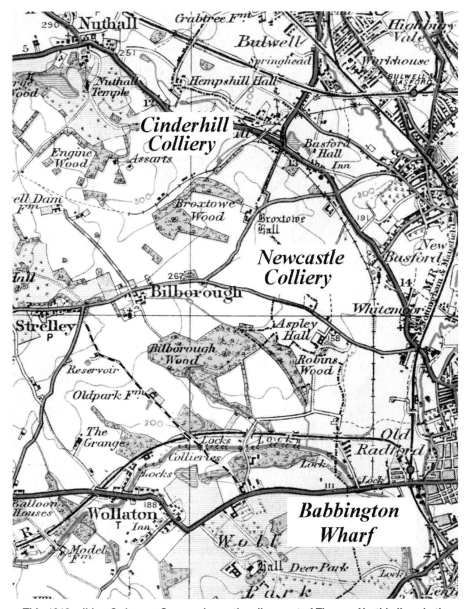

This 1918 edition Ordnance Survey shows the alignment of Thomas North's lines in the vicinity of Cinderhill The route via Newcastle Colliery south to Babbington Wharf on the Nottingham Canal was severed at Whitemoor a decade or so after the map was published, when Western Boulevard was built. The line west towards Ilkeston Junction was abandoned even earlier, and by this date only served tips to the north of Strelley village.

The dotted line shown from Strelley towards Wollaton Hall is generally thought to be the most likely route of England's first documented waggonway.

NCB Ruston & Hornsby Class LWS 0-6-0 Diesel Mechanical shunter is seen in Babbington Colliery yard, Cinderhill on 25th March 1984. Scrap wheelsets from internal user wagons can be seen amongst the general clutter in front of the locomotive. This colliery was one of several that once fed the Nottingham Mineral Railway branch to Babbington Wharf on the Nottingham Canal.

Ian Askew

Above : Moorgreen Colliery's headstocks are seen here in 1970, towering over freshly loaded BR standard 21 Ton tippler wagons. This design of vehicle was the first real advance on the traditional small capacity wagon, and was itself phased out in favour of hoppers with still greater capacity, and the ability to operate with newer large capacity loading screens.

NCB /Author's Collection

Above : Wagon labels from Nottinghamshire collieries in the 1950s hark back to a time when many thousands of wagon loads of "washed nuts" would pass through local yards like Colwick, Annesley and Toton every week.

Author's Collection

Right : Hughes 'Crab' 42763 passes Radford Colliery Sidings, on the Midland Railway's Leen Valley branch with a loaded working bound for Toton Yard. March 1959.

Tony Hill (courtesy J Bull)

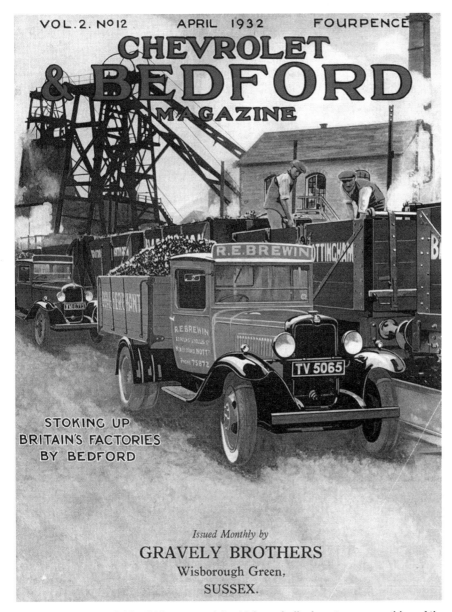

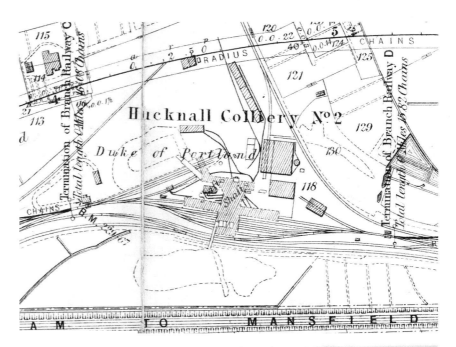

Above ; The cover of this 1932 commercial vehicle periodical captures something of the atmosphere of the pre-war Nottinghamshire coalfield.

Author's Collection

Top Right : Hucknall No 2 Colliery in 1890. Taken from a GNR land plan prepared for construction of the Leen Valley branch, it shows the colliery sandwiched between the GNR and the Midland.

Author's Collection

Above : Class 9F 92185 pulls forward from an empties rake in the reception siding at Hucknall Colliery in the early 1960s. Hucknall Town Station in the foreground had closed to passengers before the War, but continued to be used by workman's trains.

Eric Shelton

BR Class 58 No 58005 is seen approaching Sutton Hill Colliery at Stanton Hill on 20th March 1984. A Thomas Hill/Sentinel 1SDC Type4w Diesel Hydraulic shunter is visible in the background. This view was typical of the many collieries once located along the Nottinghamshire / Derbyshire border.

Ian Askew

Gedling Colliery

Gedling Colliery was not especially large, and its rail network was not particularly extensive. The Colliery was unusual however, in that the site was on a split level. The pithead, screens, reception sidings and main line connection (to the GNR Derbyshire Extension) were at the eastern end of the site, whilst the principal Landsale Wharf was located on Mapperley Plains, two hundred feet higher.

The Wharf and sidings were connected to the main complex by means of a single line cable operated incline, laid to standard gauge at a nominal 1 in 10 gradient. Loaded wagons ascended the incline, and empties were returned. The sidings at the wharf were shunted by locomotive, which itself needed to be hoisted up the incline. A variety of four and six coupled saddle tanks worked here, although those that appear to have been most photographed were Barclays "Catherine" and "Queen" of 1903 and 1923 respectively. In the late 1960s, diesel replaced steam, but the same method of working continued. Should a locomotive require a visit to the workshop for servicing, this necessitated a trip back down the incline. This operation continued until mining ceased at the site in 1990.

Two views recorded by Graham Jelly at Gedling Colliery 0n 16th July 1976.

Top : Class 20s Nos 20 063 and 20 140 stand at the head of a loaded train, ready for the return trip down the colliery branch.

Bottom : Steam lingered on at Gedling into the 1970s. Hunslet 'King George' (Works No 2409, built 1942) is seen with a selection of internal use stock.

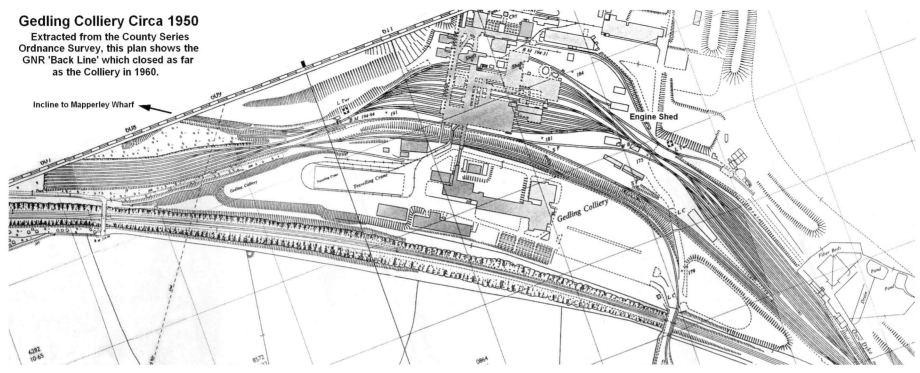

Gedling Colliery Circa 1950

Extracted from the County Series Ordnance Survey, this plan shows the GNR 'Back Line' which closed as far as the Colliery in 1960.

Incline to Mapperley Wharf →

Engine Shed

Gedling Colliery

In May 1955 an ex GCR Class O4 is seen passing Gedling Colliery with a loaded train destined for Colwick Yards. The Colliery signal box is visible in the background, marking the divergence of the colliery lines. The headstocks are also visible, and the high land of Mapperley Plains can be seen in the distance.

D R Morley / Nottingham MRS

Barclay six-coupled tank 'Catherine' of 1903 (Works No 1000) is seen shunting internal user wagons at Mapperley Landsale Wharf in 1956.

Tony Hill (Courtesy J Bull)

Two and a half decades after the previous photo, the Barclay tank has been replaced by a Thomas Hill Vanguard diesel-hydraulic shunting loco. The same old RCH designed timber built wagons were still in use however.

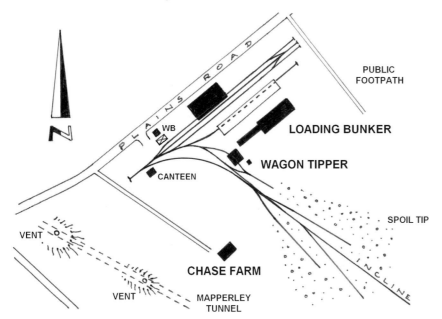

Above : A close up view of the cab of Gedling's Barclay 'Catherine', at rest between duties in the yard at Mapperley, in 1956.

Tony Hill (courtesy J Bull)

Left : A sketch of the layout of Mapperley Landsale Wharf circa 1980. The site was inaccessible to the casual photographer, and the only vantage points were the track to Chase Farm, and the public footpath towards Lambley, from which lines of crumbling wooden bodied wagons could be observed in the yard. Several of these still carried the faded letters 'Digby' on their sides, beneath the NCB lettering. These were the original colliery owners in pre-grouping times. The number of sidings had been reduced adjacent to Plains Road by the Eighties, and the original covered coaling stage was redundant and roofless. Many elements of this sketch are from memory, or taken from blurred photographs, so the author cannot claim precise accuracy in this instance.

1.2 Gypsum Workings

Gotham Hill Gypsum Tramways

These two little known narrow gauge lines date from the early years of the Twentieth Century. Little is recorded about them, and they have been overshadowed to an extent by the nearby and better known GCR standard gauge branch to Gotham from the London Extension to the east (see Volume Two). They were constructed to convey gypsum from small quarries on the north side of Gotham Hill down to barges on the River Trent. The track was built using light section flat-bottomed rail to a gauge of 2', and the lines were cheaply laid with a minimum of earthworks.

Built in 1902 by the Cafferata Company Ltd, the Barton Tramway was approximately a mile and a half in length and ran in a northerly direction. It crossed a couple of land drainage ditches, and a gated level crossing on what is today the A453, before skirting past Barton in Fabis and reaching the Trent, a little to the west. A wharf facilitated loading of the barges, which transported the gypsum downstream to Nottingham. Here it was transferred to rail, and shipped to Newark for processing into plaster. Originally the quarry kept six horses for haulage purposes, but these were replaced by a small 8hp petrol locomotive in 1912.

The Thrumpton Tramway was little more than a mile to the west, and barely a mile long. It was similar in many respects to the Barton Tramway, and seems likely operated by the same company. It ran north to a second wharf on the Trent, again crossing the present day A453 en-route to the river.

Both of the quarries closed in the early 1960s, the tracks were lifted almost immediately, and the small bridges were removed. In the early 1970s, the decaying remains of the wharf on the Trent, near Barton in Fabis were still visible, but the only clues to the existence of either tramway were the white traces of spilled gypsum visible in the soil, when the fields were ploughed, and a few bent sections of rail abandoned at the side of the public footpath leading from the A453, past Glebe Farm to Gotham Hill.

The Kingston Branch

One other tramway was built in the area to access the gypsum outcrop. The Kingston on Soar branch dated from the 1880s, and differed from the foregoing lines in that it was standard gauge with a main line connection. The quarry company owned three steam locos at various times. The Company had distinguished ownership in the form of the Lord Belper, and two of the engines carried appropriate names (Lady Margaret and Lady Angela). The line ran from the quarry at New Kingston for a distance of a little under 3 miles, before reaching the Midland Railway's main line, just north of Kegworth. Gypsum trains could often be spotted on the branch from passenger trains, atop the elevated section of the Midland's main line. A small loco shed stabled the lines motive power.

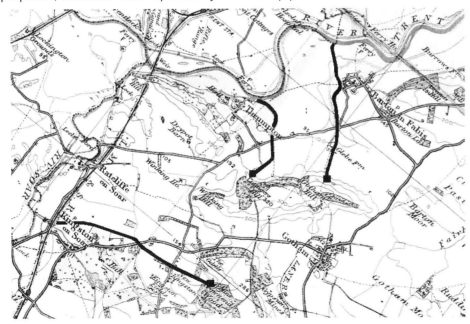

This 1930s 1" Ordnance Survey map reveals the gypsum tramways that once existed around Gotham. The lines to the north were little more than primitive plateways, carrying gypsum to barges on the Trent. The lines to the south and west were more substantial, standard gauge branches, with main line connections. The lines coveted in this volume are picked out in bold.

'Lady Angela' is seen at New Kingston in 1960. After retirement, it remained at the site in working condition, making occasional outings for enthusiasts at open days.

Rob Hancock

The last surviving steam loco on the line was Peckett 0-4-0 saddle tank 'Lady Angela'. It retired in the early 1960s to be replaced by a Ruston Diesel. This replacement locomotive had a short working life, however, as the branch closed in 1970. 'Lady Angela' has survived into preservation.

Lady Angela is seen again, in these photographs by Rob Hancock. The diminutive Peckett saddle tank is dwarfed by the BR 16 Ton mineral wagons that it is pulling in the picture above. Below the same train is captured crossing the Gotham Road.

A Tramway Surprise at Newark

A number of industrial lines grew up at Newark on Trent. The industries that supported these included engineering, brewing, brick making and gypsum extraction. Today this rail activity has vanished, and little remains to show for it. One line however was destined to give the Highway Authority a nasty surprise, almost five decades after it had closed.

The Hawton Tramway connected the Cafferata & Co. Gypsum Quarry at Hawton with Spring Wharf on the River Trent at Newark. The Company owned numerous gypsum quarries and brickyards in the Newark area. Cafferata's dense red brick facing were used extensively in eastern Nottinghamshire; the GNR Depot at Colwick being one example of their use.

The line from Hawton was built to a gauge of 3'. Initially horse-drawn, it was later operated by a pair of four-coupled saddle tanks (a Peckett and a Manning Wardle). The company also had standard gauge lines at the works, connected to the main rail network. These were worked by a variety of small tank locomotives, the last of which finished service in the early 1970s. The narrow gauge line was abandoned in 1940, however, with its two engines being sold for scrap in 1947. The rails were lifted, and the formation abandoned. The only tracks left in place were those crossing the A46 Fosse Way, which were simply surfaced over and forgotten.

These rails were 'rediscovered' in the late 1980s, when Contractors were reconstructing the road as part of work associated with building the A46 Newark Bypass. A road planing machine suffered very expensive damage when it struck the buried rails. Old maps revealed the cause and the rails were dug out. The delayed works were finished with a replacement machine.

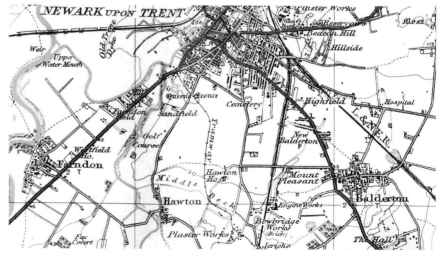

The narrow gauge tramway connecting the Hawton Works with the River Devon at Newark is seen in the centre of this 1926 edition 1 Inch Ordnance Survey map.

1.3 The Stanton Ironworks Company

Iron making was, like brick manufacturing, closely associated with mining. Furnaces sprang up close to pitheads, reducing the distance that the prodigious amounts of coal required by the furnaces needed to be moved. A string of foundries appeared along the Leen and Erewash valleys. The largest and best known was the Stanton Ironworks, near Stanton-by-Dale on the Derbyshire border. Iron founding here can trace its origins to the 1840s, but the Stanton Ironworks Company Ltd only came into existence in 1877. It grew rapidly, acquiring interests in other plants as far a field as Middlesborough, and ironstone quarries across the region. In time it became one of the largest manufacturers in the business.

The mileage of track operated by the Company was extensive, and it maintained a very substantial fleet of primarily six-coupled saddle tanks to operate its sprawling maze of sidings.

Iron founding declined after WWII, a result of cheap imports, diminishing coal reserves and changing economic trends. The Company has survived into modern times, thanks in part to timely modernisation. The manufacture of ductile iron spun pipes, drainage castings and reinforced spun concrete pipes is still undertaken at Stanton. The company still has a private rail network, but the need for a large fleet of engines has gone, and being sited close to the M1 motorway, the plant now moves much of its output by road.

Avonside saddle tank 'Stanton No 2' is seen here at the main Stanton-by-Dale site in 1955, shunting internal user wagons.

Tony Hill (Courtesy J Bull)

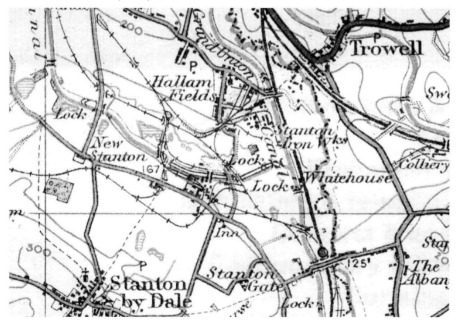

An extract from a 1920s One Inch OS plan shows how Stanton Ironworks was conveniently paced for both canal and rail access.

The Holwell Ironworks, near Melton Mowbray was part of the Stanton empire. One of their Hawthorne Leslie saddle tanks is recorded in this view dating from the early '20s

H E L Tatham

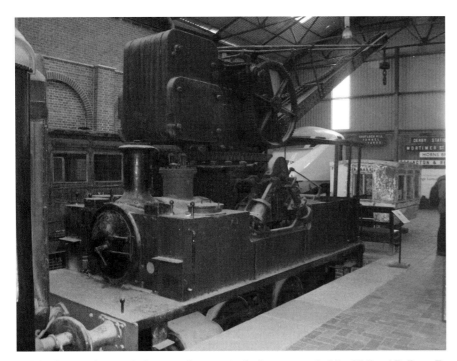

One of the Stanton Ironwork Company's crane tanks is preserved at the Midland Railway Trust, and housed at Swanwick in another relic of local railway engineering, the shed that once housed William Rigley's wagon works at Bulwell Forest.

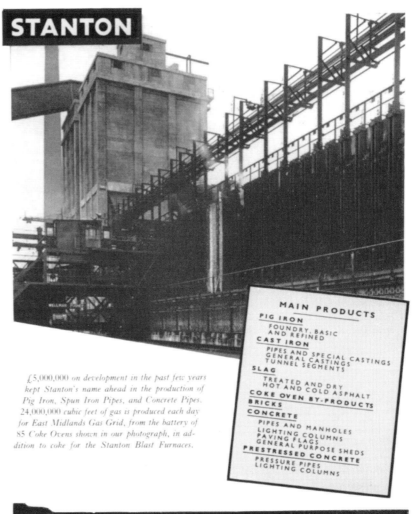

£5,000,000 on development in the past few years kept Stanton's name ahead in the production of Pig Iron, Spun Iron Pipes, and Concrete Pipes. 24,000,000 cubic feet of gas is produced each day for East Midlands Gas Grid, from the battery of 85 Coke Ovens shown in our photograph, in addition to coke for the Stanton Blast Furnaces.

MAIN PRODUCTS

PIG IRON
FOUNDRY, BASIC AND REFINED

CAST IRON
PIPES AND SPECIAL CASTINGS
GENERAL CASTINGS
TUNNEL SEGMENTS

SLAG
TREATED AND DRY
HOT AND COLD ASPHALT

COKE OVEN BY-PRODUCTS

BRICKS

CONCRETE
PIPES AND MANHOLES
LIGHTING COLUMNS
PAVING FLAGS
GENERAL PURPOSE SHEDS

PRESTRESSED CONCRETE
PRESSURE PIPES
LIGHTING COLUMNS

THE STANTON IRONWORKS COMPANY LIMITED, NEAR NOTTINGHAM. ENGLAND

Above : This company advert from 1960 features the Company's coke ovens. These liberated 'Town Gas' during the heating process, which was then supplied to the local grid. The Company continues to be an important employer, and its products are well known in the construction industry today.

Left : Sentinel 0-4-0 Diesel Hydraulic Shunting Locomotives are seen at rest at the Stanton spun pipe-works on 13th April 1986. No 62 is nearest the camera.

Ian Askew

1.4 The Nottingham Patent Brick Company

Mapperley Brickworks Tramways

The Brickworks at Mapperley trace their origins in the early part of the Nineteenth Century. They represented the only real industry in an otherwise rural area, and as the century progressed, the undulating landscape became increasingly scarred with marl pits and dotted with tall chimneys belonging to the kilns and engine houses. By the late 1870s the industry was dominated locally by the Nottingham Patent Brick Co., which had been formed in 1867, and owned a string of sites around Mapperley, Carlton and Thorneywood. The company was so successful that it went on to play a key role in the promotion of the Nottingham Suburban Railway and its Managing Director, Robert Mellors, sat on the Board of Directors of the new railway.

Construction of the Suburban Railway caused considerable disruption to the brickworks at Mapperley, with a temporary shaft sunk from the yard, to facilitate the construction of Tunnel No 3 on the line. Doubtless the clay excavated during this process found its way into the brick kilns, which in turn produced a significant proportion of the bricks used in building the railway.

Served by a railhead at Sherwood, the Mapperley Brickworks complex comprised tracks of two different gauges. A rope hauled incline from Sherwood Station yard to the kilns was built to standard gauge, with clearances for main line wagons. Sidings at the main kiln allowed the wagons to be loaded, and a stationary steam engine provided the impetus for operating the single track incline. The sidings and lines around the plant utilised wagon turntables in favour of points or curves, these being very space efficient.

Internal tramways were built to carry clay from the pits to the processing plant using a gauge of 21 inches. The internal user tub wagons were also rope hauled, being anchored at intervals onto a steel hawser. Cable shunting was not the sole means of propulsion however. Horses were used for certain operations in early years, and latterly a small four wheeled diesel locomotive operated on the site.

A number of bridges were required, and these were built using the company's own red brick. The incline was crossed by an imposing arched structure with curved wing walls, which carried the access road to the Brickworks. This seems to have been maintained by the Great Northern Railway, and it carried one of the company's cast iron bridge numbers. The road eventually became Sherwood Vale, and in the years between the Wars, housing began to appear along it. The narrow gauge lines passed beneath Woodthorpe Road, which was carried by a single span steel-beamed structure, whilst further lines burrowed deeper beneath the road in twin-bore tunnels closer to its southern end, gaining access to the excavations at the base of the escarpment. Woodthorpe Drive (originally Scout Lane) crossed a similar bridge to the Woodthorpe Road structure at the eastern extremity of the works.

A footbridge at one stage crossed the incline, part way up, but according to Ordnance Survey maps, it appears to have been removed at some time between the two World Wars. Whether this was timber or iron is unrecorded.

The excavation and conveyance of clay could be a dirty business, and in winter, the wet clay found its way over much of the site, caking the tramway wagons, tracks and hawsers.

The principal standard gauge structure on the Mapperley Brickworks complex of lines carried Sherwood Vale over the inclined plane that connected the yard on Woodborough Road with the Nottingham Suburban Railway at Sherwood Station. It is the only structure to survive intact, with other bridges having been filled in or demolished.

This print came from the collection of the late Tony Hill, a prolific local photographer who had a particular interest in the Suburban Railway. This photograph is believed to be his work and is dated 1951, by when the incline was clearly so overgrown that it must have been out of regular use for some time. The NSR finally closed to freight traffic in 1954.

Tony Hill (courtesy J Bull)

By the 1950s much of the easily accessible clay was worked out. The abandoned excavations flooded, and they became a haven for wildlife. Newts and tadpoles did particularly well in this environment, and were collected in jam jars by local children who used the site as an unofficial adventure playground.

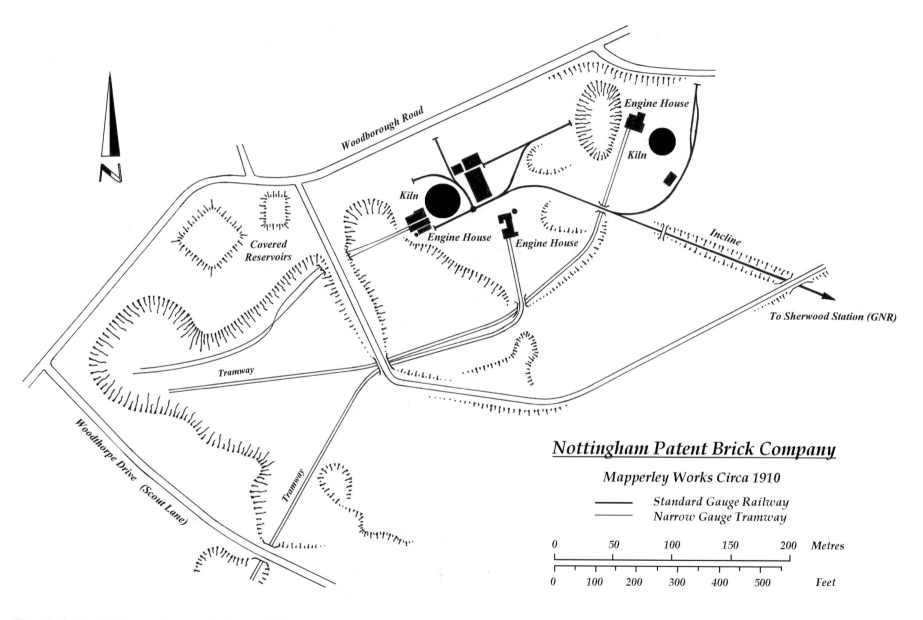

Nottingham Patent Brick Company

Mapperley Works Circa 1910

	Standard Gauge Railway
	Narrow Gauge Tramway

0   50   100   150   200   *Metres*

0   100   200   300   400   500   *Feet*

The arrival of the Nottingham Suburban Railway in 1888 was the catalyst for an expansion of operations at the Mapperley Brickworks. A second larger kiln was built, and a standard gauge rope operated incline constructed to connect the works on the top of the escarpment with the railway below. Bricks were stacked directly from the kiln into wagons, which were then winched down to Sherwood Station yard by a stationery engine. The plan above, which is based on elements of the Ordnance Survey of 1908 also shows the cable operated narrow gauge tramways that connected the brickworks with the clay pits. Stationary steam engines provided the power for these tramways. Today the brickworks site is occupied by a car dealership, and the clay pits have been redeveloped for housing.

The incline from Sherwood Station to Mapperley Brickworks is seen here in 1955. The rails had been lifted a year or so before this photograph, and nature has started to reclaim the formation, doubtless assisted by scant maintenance in the immediate years before closure. The incline was progressively filled over and reclaimed, with local residents incorporating much of it into their gardens. Some of the alignment still survives however, covered with dense undergrowth.

Tony Hill (Courtesy J Bull)

The Mapperley site was progressively abandoned and its dwindling output transferred to road haulage after the Suburban Railway closed. The Brickworks were closed in the late 1960s, and over the next decade much of it was reclaimed for housing, vehicle retail and associated storage compounds. Today, the irregular landform, with massive cuts into the hillside, betrays the area's industrial past. Other smaller scale reminders can still be found however. The lower portion of the incline to Sherwood Station still exists, albeit heavily overgrown, and the arched bridge still carries Sherwood Vale across the alignment. The site of the top of the incline and loading sidings also survives, but is buried in undergrowth, and hidden behind a boundary fence of a car dealership that occupies much of the site.

The excavations to the east of Woodthorpe Drive have been landscaped to create playing fields, but the parapets of the bridge that carried the road across the tramway can still be seen, although the structure was under filled by the County Council in the late nineties. The Woodthorpe Road bridge has also been filled in, but again the parapets of this are still visible. The neighbouring twin tunnels have also been buried, but the steepness of the bank overhanging the filled portals has left a legacy of slope stability problems, responsibility for which has passed to the Highway Authority, since the residual bank supports the public highway.

The south elevation of the bridge over the rope worked incline was perhaps less attractive than the north side, lacking the nicely proportioned sweeping wing walls, and being generally shorter, due to rising ground levels. By 1968, the narrow steep cutting was partially filled with erosion material, together with fly tipped spoil. The flats in the background occupy the site of the station yard and exchange sidings for the brickworks. Today this view is completely obscured by trees and dense undergrowth.

Tony Hill (Courtesy J Bull)

The Thorneywood Brickworks

Again owned by the Nottingham Patent Brick Company, this site was also close to the line of the Nottingham Suburban Railway. In common with the Mapperley Works, the yard was connected to the main line railway by means of a standard gauge single track rope-hauled incline, although it was not as steep as the one at Mapperley. The distinguishing feature of this however was that it passed through tunnel for much of its length, beneath Porchester Road and Burgass Road. A series of sidings provided loading facilities, and a single cylinder 150HP horizontal steam engine provided power for the winches and crushing machinery.

Narrow gauge tramways connected the processing plant with the marl pits, and like at Mapperley, these were cable operated by steam winding engines. The lack of public thoroughfares meant however that no structures were required, and consequently the lightly built tramway was relayed several times, to suit the changing needs of the clay extraction operation. The operations at Thorneywood were larger than those at Mapperley, and the company operated two large kilns here. The extent of clay extraction was more extensive, and large tracts of land were rendered desolate wasteland over the century or more of operation.

By the time this 1955 view was recorded, the last remnants of the Nottingham Suburban Railway had been abandoned, and the rails serving Thorneywood Brickworks had been lifted. The tunnel leading from the station yard, beneath Porchester Road, towards the Brickyards has today been filled over, and no trace can be seen.

Photo Tony Hill (Courtesy J Bull)

At its peak output, the brickworks generated a considerable volume of traffic, and the Company's loaded wagons could be seen lined up in Thorneywood Station Yard, awaiting dispatch across the country.

The winding engine at Thorneywood initially operated the Brickworks processing plant, and the hawsers that hauled the tub wagons around the narrow gauge rail system at the site. With the coming of the Nottingham Suburban Railway in 1888, it performed a new function, hauling standard gauge open wagons from Thorneywood Station yard, up an underground incline, to the Company's yard on Burgass Road. Today this impressive piece of engineering can be seen at Nottingham's Industrial Museum, at Wollaton Hall. Here it is undergoing long term restoration by Arkwright Society volunteers, and will hopefully one day work again.

The Nottingham Patent Brick Company did not have a monopoly at Thorneywood, and a smaller competitor operated from a site to the south of Carlton Road. The Nottingham Builders Brick Company was a much smaller operation, without the complex network of tramways and inclines employed by its neighbour. This short lived brickworks was served by a siding from the Suburban line, and appears to have closed some time around The Great War.

Brick production ceased at Thorneywood in the late 1960s, although rail shipment of the company's products had ended in 1954, when the Suburban line closed. The site was cleared, and much of it lay waste for years, before housing estates grew up. One surviving curiosity is the principal winding engine. When the engine house was demolished, the engine and its foundations were carefully left in place, and incorporated into a new public house, as a feature. For two decades the engine provided a talking point for the hostelry, before the pub was in turn remodelled and its industrial heritage discarded. The engine was fortunately donated by Shipstones Brewery to the City's Industrial Museum at Wollaton Hall, where it is being gradually restored by volunteers from the Nottingham Arkwright Society.

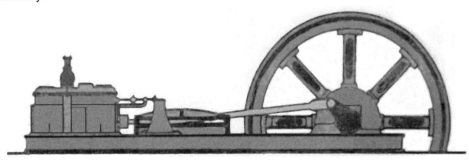

The Thorneywood engine is thought to have been manufactured by Tangyes of Birmingham in about 1850. It is likely to have been used at a colliery, before the Nottingham Patent Brick Company bought it second hand in from a local dealer in 1867. Its single cylinder is 23inch diameter, and it worked at a pressure of 100psi to deliver 150HP, equivalent to the output of a modern large car engine.

Illustration Nottingham City Council

1.5 Nottingham Corporation Rail Connections

Through the latter years of the Nineteenth Century, and the first part of the Twentieth Century, the Corporation of the City of Nottingham evolved into a large and multi-faceted operation. It was responsible for a vast range of services and amenities, which included water supply and sewage disposal, manufacture and supply of gas, generation of electricity, operation of trams and omnibuses, and maintaining roads, bridges, civic buildings and hospitals. To support this wide range of infrastructure, maintenance depots were distributed around the City. Many of these were rail served.

Gasworks Rail Connections

In 1874 control was vested with the Nottingham Corporation of the City's gasworks. The primary gas production facilities were located at Eastcroft and Basford, with a smaller facility at Radford. Town Gas was produced at these sites by heating coal in sealed retorts, to drive off the gas. This produced coke as by-products, together with tar and ammonia. Large quantities of coal and coke needed to be moved around the sites, and liquid tar, coke and ash needed to be transported away. Consequently a substantial network of sidings and tracks grew up within each site.

The Eastcroft Gasworks were the most centrally located of the City's plants, close to the GNR sidings at London Road. Rail access was taken from the rear of the goods yard, and a canal wharf lay to the north. The northern side of the site was crossed in 1898 by the connecting line from Trent Lane to Weekday Cross and the GCR. The new railway was elevated for its entire length, and placed on steel trestles with offset piers were it spanned the gasworks sidings. Tar from the Eastcroft Gasworks was transported to the Corporations highways depot, on the opposite side of the Midland Railway lines, and was used, together with ash and coke residue in the construction and repair of roads.

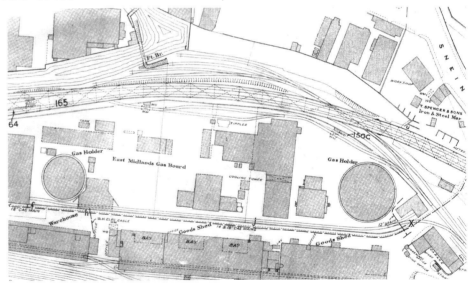

Eastcroft Gasworks was sandwiched between the GNR and the Nottingham Canal. Over the century or so that it existed, it was remodelled a number of times, and ownership passed from the City Corporation with Nationalisation in 1947. Rail access was taken from the east of the site, and reception sidings were laid out to the north, adjacent to the canal. These were worked by a four wheel Peckett saddle tank belonging to the gasworks. In 1898 the GN constructed an elevated line across the sidings, to connect with the GCR's London Extension and Victoria Station. The plan is taken from 1950s BR record drawings.

Author's Collection

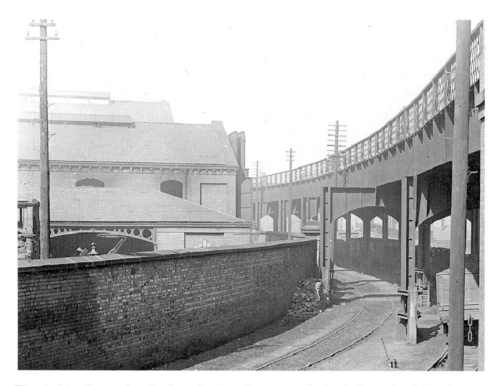

The steel trestle carrying the Great Northern line across Eastcroft Gasworks sidings is seen here in 1904 in an official railway company photograph. The lines of wooden bodied wagons in the shadows below would have conveyed coal to the Gasworks from the collieries of the Leen and Erewash valleys. A set of lines cross the sidings at right angles, in the shadows beneath the projecting trestle, before passing through a gap in the wall behind the pillar. Wagons in the sidings were uncoupled and placed over wagon turntables, before being shunted into the plant along these feeder lines.

Author's Collection

Basford Gasworks was built alongside the Midland Railway's Leen Valley branch in the 1860s, on Radford Road, and it was serviced by sidings from that line. Within the site, the retorts were fed by numerous lines and spurs. A further line led to an ash dump at the southern extremity of the site. In common with other industrial complexes, wagon turntables were used, owing to the confined space. Various steam haulage was used to move wagons, and in latter years, a pair of Peckett-built, four-coupled saddle tank locomotives were employed at the site.

Radford Gasworks was also built next to the same line, and located to the east side of it. It was sited between Lenton and Radford stations, close to what is now Triumph Road. The modern gasometers that remain nearby are a clue to the history of the area. A single line fed into the gasworks site from the down line, and a run-round loop was provided in the yard. Wagon turntables on the reception road allowed individual wagons to be taken out of the arriving formation, and hauled into

the retort buildings for discharge. Production of Town Gas ceased at the site after the Second World War, and today, the area is occupied by a housing estate and nothing of the original gasworks is left to see.

Control of gas manufacturing and its distribution passed from the Local Authority on 1st May 1949 to the newly created East Midlands Gas Board. The discovery of North Sea gas in the 1960s spelt the end of traditional gasworks. Almost overnight the industry disappeared. Eastcroft gasworks were demolished in around 1970, and much of the equipment at Basford was removed at the same time. The only remaining part of the Eastcroft gasworks at the time of writing is the boundary wall to the south of the site. The warehouse that was built over the site has also now been demolished, and the site is destined for redevelopment as a mixed residential and employment area. One legacy that the Developers will have to contend with is cleaning up ground contamination, which includes a range of toxic by-products resulting from a century of Town Gas production.

East Midland Gas continued to use the Basford site as a depot for another 20 years, without a rail connection, and the gasholders remain in service to this day. The gasworks ash dump at Basford has subsequently become the site of the NET tram depot, and a fresh form of rail use has returned to the site.

The Retort House at the preserved Fakenham Gasworks in North Norfolk gives an idea of both the processes involved, and the appearance of a Victorian Gasworks. This is the only surviving plant in England, and the retorts, in which the coal was burned, are pictured here. The coal was burned in a low oxygen environment, to liberate the gas. The Nottingham Corporation employed similar plant at its gasworks, and the interior of the City's retort houses would originally have appeared very similar.

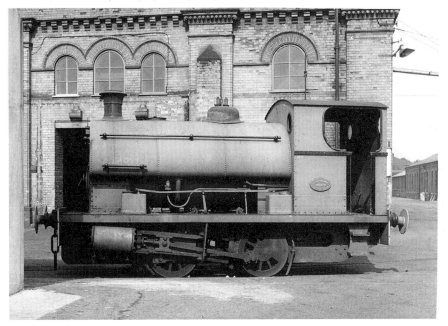

The end of the preserved Retort House at Fakenham, and part of the condensing plant that separated ammonia from the raw gas are seen above. The Retort houses at Basford were considerably larger, and the view below shows Peckett Works No 1879 stood alongside one. This engine was one of two saddle tanks used by Basford Gasworks at this time, and it was photographed by Tony Hill in 1966.

By 1996, the retorts at Basford had been long demolished, and nature had taken over. Some of the rails were still in place, but little else remained to be seen. Part of the site was subsequently used for the construction of the depot for the NET light rail system.

Corporation Depots

The Nottingham Corporation had numerous depots and facilities spread around the City, and a number of these were rail served.

Eastcroft Depot on London Road once had an extended private siding running through the length of the site, from the Midland Railway, by London Road Junction. It terminated in a fan of three roads at the Corporation's canal basin to the south of the site, and a passing loop at the refuse destructor allowed open wagons to be loaded and unloaded at the incinerator, without obstructing the site. Individual wagons were horse shunted, and loads included aggregates, timber, tar and dressed granite from the Mountsorrel quarries in Leicestershire. Maintenance equipment and rails for the Corporations tram system were also delivered here, with track components coming from Sheffield manufacturers. In the late 19th Century, less savoury materials loaded here included night soil, for transfer to Stoke Bardolph.

The Corporation also owned the City's Cattle Market, and the cattle docks that served it. These were also fed by sidings connected to the Midland at London Road Junction, and from these, a pair of lines kicked back into the timber yard of Ashworth, Kirk. These sidings would have been locomotive worked by the Midland Railway, and the track geometry and turnout radii was consequently more generous than the Sanitary Depot siding.

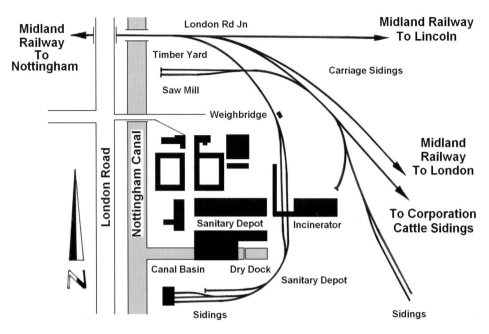

The Nottingham Corporation once had numerous rail connections in the Eastcroft area. The maintenance depot was served by private sidings and a canal basin, and the neighbouring refuse incinerator also had its own siding. The Corporation owned the City's Cattle Market and this too had a number of private sidings.

Other Corporation depots were also rail served. A short spur from the south end of Bulwell Market Station yard, on the Midland Railway's Leen Valley branch crossed the River Leen to serve a small depot on Coventry Road, whilst the Corporation depot on Western Boulevard at Basford, to the south of Basford Vernon Station also had its own siding. After the Second World War, improved road vehicles became available. Investment in roads was not matched with investment in the railways, and it became increasingly difficult for rail transport to match its economic and flexible competition. The Corporation progressively switched delivery of materials to road transport, and by 1960, its depots were no longer rail served.

Sewage Trains

Raw materials were not the only product shipped by rail for the Corporation, or necessitating private sidings. Until the creation of Severn-Trent Water in 1960, water treatment plants were operated by the Authority, and these included the City's main sewage treatment plant at Stoke Bardolph, which opened in the 1880s. In the years before the construction of the trunk sewer alongside the Midland's Lincoln line, sewage was conveyed by "Night Soil" train from London Road Goods Yard to a private siding on the eastern side of Colwick Yards. Crossing the Ouse Dyke by the Engineers sidings, the line fed into the treatment plant, and a narrow

gauge system transported waste around the site. Separated solids were transported in tippler wagons to Stoke Farm, where they would be ploughed into the fields by the Plant's two mighty Fowler ploughing engines (both of which are preserved). In latter years the system was operated by a Simplex four wheeled locomotive.

As the City infrastructure developed, sewers replaced the night soil trains. The standard gauge siding was finally abandoned in the 1950s. With modernisation of the water treatment plant, the narrow gauge railway system was also eventually abandoned and the locomotive retired to the Midland Railway Centre at Butterley, together with two of the tippler wagons. Today scant evidence remains on site of this narrow gauge railway.

The Midland Railway Centre at Butterley is home to an interesting collection of retired industrial rolling stock. The Ruston locomotive formerly belonged to Severn Trent, and the tippler wagons were once used at Stoke Bardolph Sewage Works.

Hospital Sidings

Today it seems unlikely that a City Corporation might run hospitals, serviced by private railway sidings, but that is precisely the situation that existed in the late Nineteenth Century. In the 1890s the Nottingham Corporation built a Workhouse, Infirmary and Isolation Hospital for infectious diseases in the then rural setting of Basford. The new facility replaced the old Workhouse that had been demolished to make way for the Great Central Railway's Nottingham Victoria Station

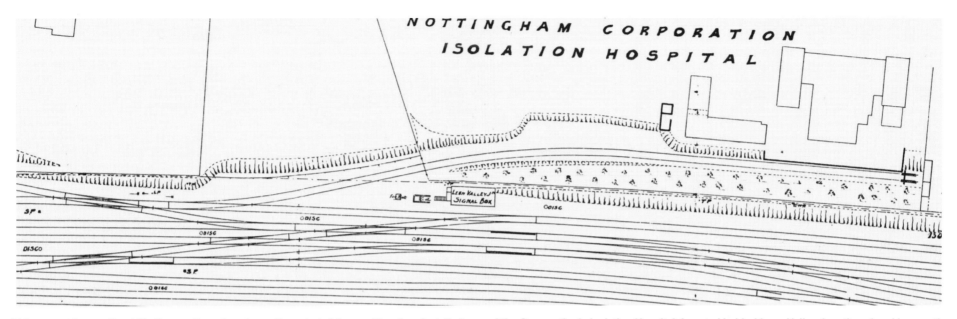

NOTTINGHAM CORPORATION
ISOLATION HOSPITAL

This extract from a Great Northern rating plan shows the gated siding and loading dock that served the Corporation's Isolation Hospital. Located behind Leen Valley Junction signal box on the Derbyshire Extension, it is likely that it provided the means of bringing construction materials in during construction, as well as consumables. The siding fell out of use before the Second World War, and the site of it and the railway have now been lost beneath development.

The new site bounded the Great Northern Railway's Derbyshire Extension, and private sidings were built immediately behind the Leen Valley Junction signal box.

These sidings were likely used for delivering construction materials, but once the hospitals were complete, they would have provided a convenient way of bringing in bulky consumables such as the coal required to run the heating boilers.

Many of the original Workhouse and Isolation Hospital buildings survive as part of the present day City Hospital, but the sidings were abandoned before the Second World War, and today nothing remains of them or indeed the neighbouring railway line.

North Wilford Power Station

North Wilford Power Station was another Corporation asset with a private rail facility, and dated from the early 1930s. Built to supply the City's growing demand for electricity, it was sited adjacent to Clifton Colliery and alongside the Midland line into Nottingham from Lenton South Junction. The colliery was primarily served by the LMS, but also had a connection to the rival LNER's Queens Walk Goods Yard. The relative locations of Clifton Colliery and North Wilford Power Station meant that coal could be moved from one to the other, without travelling on public railways.

North Wilford Power Station dominates the skyline in this 1981 photograph recording the reconstruction of Wilford Toll Bridge. A few years after this view was taken, the power station was closed and demolished.

Nottingham City Council

A series of internal lines connected the two and unusually, some of the power station lines were electrified. Whilst details on this system are scant, it seems probable that it worked on similar principles to the Corporation's tramway system, operating with direct current picked the power up from overhead contact wires and the current returned via the rails. It is known that four wheeled steam locomotives were used, and presumably the electric locos were the same wheel configuration.

With nationalisation of the power industry in 1948, North Wilford passed from Corporation ownership to the newly formed East Midlands Electricity Board.

The electric locomotives were supplemented with a variety of steam locomotives, including a fireless loco and a couple of 0-4-0 Pecketts. The neighbouring colliery operated 'Austerities' in their yards into the late 'Sixties and these were destined to become the last steam locomotives to regularly work within the boundaries of the City of Nottingham.

The closure of Clifton Colliery saw a change in the way that the power station was serviced, with coal now brought in from the adjacent Midland line being used to fuel it. This method of supply continued until North Wilford Power Station was closed and demolished in the early 1980s. Today no trace remains of it, or the private railways that served it.

1.6 The Boots Company

One of the City's most famous manufacturing names is the Boots Company. Founded by Jesse Boot as the Boots Pure Drug Company in the 1870s, the company swiftly grew to become a market leader, and several manufacturing facilities were built on the southern fringe of the City, in the vicinity of Island Street, Station Street and the Nottingham Canal.

In 1932, the company expanded, and invested in what was for the time, one of the most advanced facilities in Europe. Located at Beeston, just outside the City boundary, the revolutionary manufacturing and warehousing complex was laid out in a spacious and modern industrial estate, the likes of which had not been seen before in this Country. The centrepiece of the site was the D34 block, an airy and well designed structure that placed unprecedented emphasis on the comfort of the Company's workers.

The site was bounded by the LMS Derby line to the north, and the Beeston Canal to the south. A standard gauge private railway looped around the Boots site, and connected to exchange sidings.

The Boots Company operated a pair of fireless locomotives, built by Andrew Barclay of Kilmarnock. These unusual locomotives ran on steam generated from a charge of pressurised superheated water, injected into an insulated tank that took the place of a conventional boiler. A locomotive would run for several hours on a single charge, depending on the amount of work being done. Prior to the Great War, the patent to this method of propulsion was held by a German company.

This 1950s Boots publicity photograph from a contemporary City Council publication shows the view south along Main Road. The private railway ran to the right of the road, and exchange sidings lay behind the trees in the extreme right of the photograph. Lines crossed it into the side roads alongside the building blocks. Covered railway wagons can be seen in the background, behind the Employee's bus that is emerging from Third Avenue. This development was architecturally and structurally significant, and both building blocks in this view now enjoy listed status.

Author's Collection

The surrender of patent rights after the war opened the market up to British manufacturers. Use of these diminutive four-coupled engines ensured that the site was clean and free from smoke, soot, and coal dust, a positive advantage when engaged in the manufacture of pharmaceuticals and cosmetics. Fire risk was also eliminated with this type of locomotives - several large paper mills around the country used them. In addition to the fireless locos, from 1944 the Company owned a conventional Barclay four wheel saddle tank (Works No 2166).

As well as the standard gauge lines, the Company operated a narrow gauge line that transferred waste materials to a tipping site on the east side of the plant. This ran in a southerly arc from the end of Sixth Avenue.

The Boots system operated successfully for 25 years, but in 1955 an event took place that was to mark a turning point in the fortunes of rail operation. A strike by footplatemen on British Railways that year created massive disruption in the delivery of goods by rail. The Company's Despatch Manager at that time, Mr Harold Stones was faced with a stark choice; either see Boots fail to honour its deliveries, or seek alternative means. Road haulage contractors were called in and after discussion, agreed, not only to ship goods normally sent by rail, but to deliver next day to the customers' doorstep.

Photographed at the entrance to Boots factory sidings at Beeston, is Stanier 2-cylinder 2-6-4 tank No 42588 of Nottingham Shed. This scene was recorded in April 1964. The road entrance to the site and the gatehouse can be seen in the background, together with one of the company's distinctive concrete lamp posts.

Michael Stones

The Railway was unable to deliver the flexibility of road transport, and after the strike had finished, contracts for moving products by rail were progressively discarded and road transport took over. The internal rail system continued to operate until the Seventies, but transport of goods by the national rail network ceased entirely in the late Sixties. After the internal network closed, Boots donated the locomotives to preservation groups, and the lines were abandoned.

Boots No 1 went to the Foxfield Railway in Staffordshire, and its sister engine No 2 found a closer home at the Midland Railway Centre, at Butterley in Derbyshire. The lack of a conventional boiler means that neither locomotive are likely to run again, but both will continue to provide long term reminders of one of Nottingham's most unusual and forward thinking industrial sites.

Boots Fireless locomotive No 2 is today preserved at the Midland Railway Centre, near Ripley in Derbyshire. The locomotive has been restored to Boots corporate blue. Unlike more conventional industrial locomotives, the two outside cylinders are located beneath the cab floor.

Ex-Midland 4F No 43954 is seen here in Boots factory sidings in March 1964. The locomotive was allocated to Nottingham Shed for many years. The roof line of one of the factory units can be seen in the background.

Michael Stones

The rails around the site were progressively lifted after operation of the line ceased, and after a series of changes of Company ownership, today production has been moved away. 80 years after its construction, a large part of the site lies quiet, and all that is left of the private railway are a series of connected open spaces, car parks and roadways that once comprised the route.

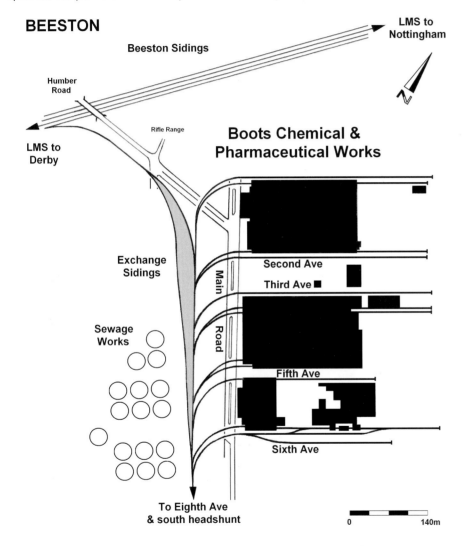

BEESTON

LMS to Nottingham

Beeston Sidings

Humber Road

Rifle Range

LMS to Derby

Boots Chemical & Pharmaceutical Works

Main Road

Exchange Sidings

Second Ave

Third Ave ■

Sewage Works

Fifth Ave

Sixth Ave

To Eighth Ave & south headshunt

0   140m

Above : The schematic layout shows the layout of the Boots plant at Beeston as it appeared just before the Second World War. Trains were deposited and assembled in the exchange sidings, and the Company's shunting locomotives moved the wagons around the various sites to be loaded or unloaded. Today, the site seems destined for redevelopment, and one possibility being explored is to convert the grade II listed D34 block into a shopping centre.

Boots Fireless No 2 is again seen here at the Midland Railway Centre. The locomotive has been attractively restored, but the livery is not strictly authentic. When in service, it didn't carry the company logo, and the pressure cylinder end was painted with wasp stripes. The shed in which it is housed is another relic of Nottingham's industrial railways, being formerly located at William Rigley's Bulwell Forest wagon works.

The son of Boots' Despatch Manager, David Stones, spent some of his formative years observing train movements into and out of the site, in the years following the Second World War. Appendix 1 contains an account of his recollections of railway operation here, from the 1940s, through to the end of operation.

1.7 Beeston Creosote Works

Another industrial oddity once existed but a stones throw from the Boots complex. The Midland Railway constructed a 3' gauge system to service its creosote works adjacent to Beeston Sidings, to the north of the line to Derby. The works were built to treat railway sleepers and these were conveyed through large cylindrical retorts on low narrow gauge wagons. Once inside, the chambers were sealed and the timbers (and wagons) were pressure impregnated. After treatment, the sleepers were transferred by steam crane into the stackyard, or for shipment onto wagons on standard gauge tracks alongside, but several feet lower than the works system.

The Creosote plant appears to have been operated by several different locomotives during its 80 or so years of life. The earliest documented engine (although not the first) was a six coupled Manning-Wardle saddle tank named 'Danby Lodge', which was built in 1903, and discarded in the 1930s. In LMS and early BR days, four wheeled Fowler internal combustion locos, variously either ED2/ED5 plus others were used to work the standard gauge sidings alongside to narrow gauge system. Following WW2, two 0-4-0 saddle tanks were used on the narrow gauge system. The first of these was named 'Batley', which lasted from 1945 until 1956. This was replaced by 'No 1', a small Bagnall outside cylinder locomotive dating from 1911. No 1 was replaced in 1958 by a diesel locomotive, which worked the plant until closure.

The works fell out of use in the mid 1960s as a consequence the shrinking rail network, and falling demand for timber sleepers. Within a year or two the site of the works was cleared to make way for another of Dr Beeching's legacies, a new freightliner depot. Thus the creosote works and its narrow gauge railway system was consigned to the history book.

Top : The 3' Gauge shunter 'Batley' is seen at Beeston Creosote Works on 28th April 1946. The works mobile steam crane is visible behind the locomotive.

David Stones Collection

Below : This 1957 view from 'Boots Bridge' shows Britannia Pacific 70017 'Arrow' heading a Nottingham Midland - St Pancras express past Beeston Sidings. Creosote Works' sleeper stackyard is visible in the background, and the building above Arrow's chimney is the brick built engine shed. By this date 'Batley ' had been withdrawn.

Michael Stones

The Beeston Creosote Works are visible on this 1920s 1 Inch OS Map. The tramway is to the north of the sidings, and lines serving the sleeper stacks are perpendicular to the main yard.

1.8 The Trent Navigation Company

Tucked away from public view, the Trent Basin lies a short distance to the south of Daleside Road. Built in the early 1930s by the Trent Navigation Company, when commercial traffic on the River Trent was still economically viable, the basin was one of three 'waterhead' depots in the City. It was (and indeed still is) 300' x100', with sufficient depth to take the heaviest barges that then operated on the river, the draught of which could be in excess of six feet. A 400' long wharf fronted the river, and distinctive flat roofed four-storey warehouses were constructed in reinforced concrete, adjacent to both the wharf and the basin. The warehouse adjacent to the river was built by the Nottingham Corporation.

The site incorporated grain silos and six ton cranes for unloading merchandise. In the 1950s, a suction lift was added, to assist in unloading grain cargoes. The warehouses were rail served by standard gauge sidings, each provided with a run round loop. The western side of the basin had a siding immediately alongside the berths, with its own loop. To the east of the basin, the Company constructed a small single road engine shed. What type of locomotive was housed here is unrecorded, but the short trains dictated by the loop lengths and tight curves of the lines serving the Basin and the modest proportions of the shed suggest a short wheelbase four coupled tank, or perhaps early internal combustion powered loco.

The sidings converged to the north of the basin, and a single track branch crossed Daleside Road, running into exchange sidings laid parallel to and south of the LMS route to Lincoln. The junction for the Exchange Sidings lay a short distance east of Meadow Lane, and was controlled from nearby Sneinton Junction Signal Box.

The basin and its rail connection probably saw most use in the war years, but commercial use of the River Trent fell into decline in the years that followed. Nationalisation of the industry and the creation of the British Waterways Board did little to help, and by the 1960s, the rail connection to the Basin had been abandoned and remaining incoming traffic was routed by road via Trent Lane.

The decline of commercial traffic and lack of capital for investment meant that the Trent Basin facilities remained substantially as built right up to their disposal, by BWB in 1988. At this time, railway tracks that had not been used for nearly three decades, remained mostly in situ, together with the engine shed and warehousing.

The fast growing property market of the early 21st Century has meant that redundant industrial assets have come under increasing threat of redevelopment. Trent Basin is one such site, with attractive views across the river providing a strong selling point. The local authority was keen to see this area of derelict site redeveloped, and Planning Consent was granted for a major residential development in 2007. Exactly when this project moves forward will depend on national economic factors and the buoyancy of the development market in Nottingham.

When redevelopment eventually takes place, this obscure piece of Nottingham's transport history and the City's last remaining freight interchange point between water and rail will disappear.

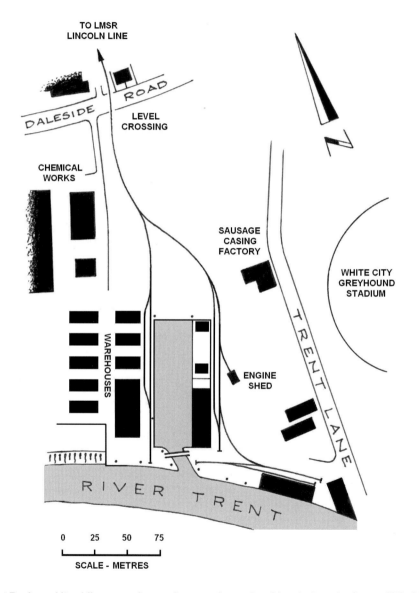

Trent Basin and its sidings are shown above as they existed just before the Second World War. The plan was prepared using information taken from County Series Ordnance Survey mapping. By the time 1960s editions were published, the railway had been deleted from the maps, indicating its abandonment. Despite plan evidence, many of the lines still existed in 2009.

The gently decaying remains of Trent Basin are seen here in January 2009. Proposed redevelopment of the site would see all the original buildings demolished.

Above : Abandoned railway lines disappear into the scrub. The rail section is grooved tramway rail, similar in section to types illustrated on page 83.

Right : The line leading to the engine shed was still in place in January 2009. The shed itself is a simple brick built structure, with a flat roof, although this is likely to be a replacement for an earlier roof, with ventilators for the locomotive's exhaust.

1.9 The Colwick Estates Light Railway

The Colwick Estates Light Railway, built by the Great Northern Railway, was opened in 1919. It provided rail access to the growing industrial area to the south the Company's Nottingham–Grantham line close to its marshalling yard at Colwick.

A junction was constructed by Colwick East Junction Signal Box, and exchange sidings built alongside the Grantham line. The principal line ran alongside the private road through the estate and was mostly double tracked when first built. Ungated crossings abounded on the line, and there would eventually be something like two dozen. Private sidings led off the line to a diverse range of companies.

Timber, aggregate, animal feed and engineering products traffic was generated along the line, but the most important products to use the line were probably petrochemicals and sugar beet. The Anglo-Scottish Beet Sugar Corporation (Latterly the British Sugar Corporation) built a processing plant alongside the River Trent, and this grew to be one of the largest in the region. At its peak, the plant was capable of handling and processing 200 wagon loads of sugar beet every day. To handle this, the company operated three saddle tanks (two Pecketts and a Hudswell Clarke), together with a rail mounted steam crane, and latterly a small diesel shunter. Rail deliveries of sugar beet continued to the plant until the 1970s, when remaining traffic switched to road haulage. For the next decade, the sidings were left to rust, and the remaining rolling stock on site progressively decayed. Processing at Colwick did not have long to survive, and today much of the Sugar Beet Factory lies derelict and disintegrating, and the greater part of the site is used as a trailer park.

From the 1920s, Colwick Estate became increasingly important for petrol storage and petroleum products were delivered by both rail tanker and barge from the River Trent. Petrochemical companies are still users of the site, although on a reduced scale.

Concrete product manufacturing has also long been associated with the estate, and the Trent Concrete Company also had private sidings, worked by a trio of four-coupled saddle tanks, of varied and ancient origin. The plant was connected to quarries on the east side of the GNR's Grantham line by a 15" gauge tramway. These rail operations were abandoned in the sixties, but concrete products are still manufactured at Colwick today.

The branch was worked in steam days by typically six-coupled saddle tanks, from the neighbouring Colwick Depot. They were phased out in the late 1950s to be replaced by English Electric diesel-electric shunters. Latterly denoted Class 08, these shunters operated the line in its declining years. Sadly, as goods traffic switched to cheaper and more flexible road transport in the 1950s and 1960s, the need for a rail system to distribute materials and products around the estate diminished. Class A petrochemicals continued to be delivered to the site to the last. In 1985 a new unloading terminal was constructed to the north side of the Grantham line, and the Colwick Estates Light Railway closed.

BR Class 08 0-6-0DE No. 08858 shunting 4w TTA tank wagons at the Shell Mex/BP oil depot on the Colwick Estates Light Railway, 25th September 1984

Ian Askew

The lines lingered on for a few years after closure, but today, most of the rail has been recovered. The industrial estate has undergone many changes in the intervening years but much of the physical route has survived. A few reminders can still be found, including a number of truncated rail sections at the site of road crossings, and most surprisingly, a level crossing sign remains in place at one location, almost 25 years after the last train passed.

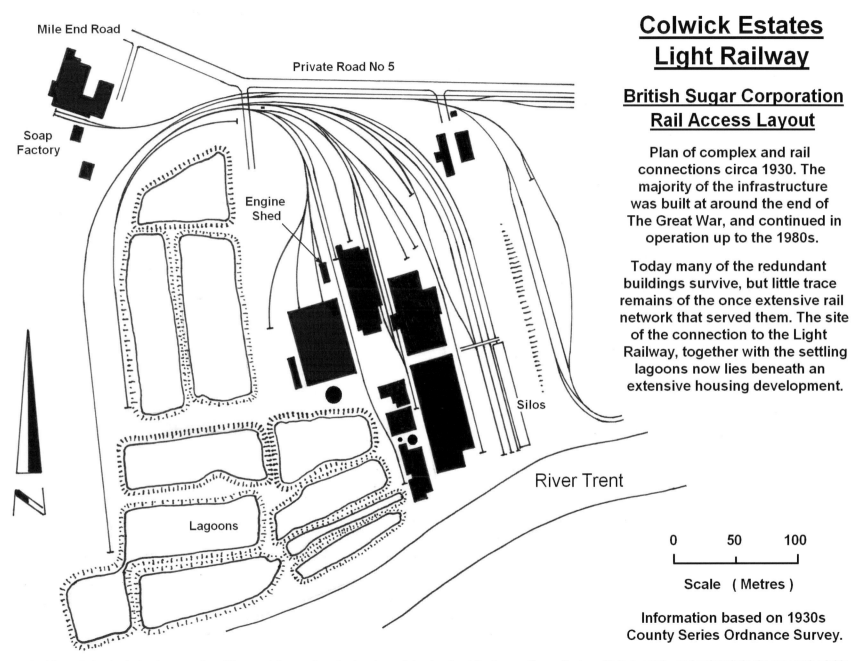

Colwick Estates Light Railway

British Sugar Corporation Rail Access Layout

Plan of complex and rail connections circa 1930. The majority of the infrastructure was built at around the end of The Great War, and continued in operation up to the 1980s.

Today many of the redundant buildings survive, but little trace remains of the once extensive rail network that served them. The site of the connection to the Light Railway, together with the settling lagoons now lies beneath an extensive housing development.

Mile End Road

Private Road No 5

Soap Factory

Engine Shed

Silos

River Trent

Lagoons

0   50   100

Scale (Metres)

Information based on 1930s County Series Ordnance Survey.

The Author had intended to include photographs of the surviving engine shed and remaining tracks at the former Sugar Factory. Unfortunately, and uniquely in the research of this series of books, the owners would not give consent for them to be photographed. The site is currently for sale, with a view to demolition and redevelopment.

08 856 is seen at the western end of the remaining line on 23rd March 1985. By this time, the lines to the British Sugar plant had been lifted, and buffer stops erected part way along Private Road No 5.

Graham Jelly

The Shell Mex plant is seen here on 28th March 1985. 08 856 is propelling a rake of 45 tonne tankers into the site on the penultimate day of rail operation.

Graham Jelly

08 856 is seen at the eastern end of the Estates Railway on 29th March 1985, en-route to collect the very last regular working on the line. The GNR route to Grantham is in the background.

Graham Jelly

Class 08 No 08858 was a regular performer on the Colwick Estates Light Railway. It is seen here propelling an air braked guards van across the Private Road No 3 crossing in May 1979. This trip had seen a short rake of Class A TTA tank wagons delivered to the Shell-Mex / BP petrochemical storage plant. *Author*

37 022 hurries past 08 741 at the Estates Railway junction with a Harwich-Manchester boat train in March 1985. *Graham Jelly*

25 152 propels a permanent way train along the Colwick Estates Railway on 10/11/79. *Graham Jelly*

The last revenue earning train, an empty rake of TTA Class A tanks, leaves the Estate Railway on 29th March 1985, in the charge of 31 161. *Graham Jelly*

2.0 Nottingham and the Preservation Era

Museums, Heritage Railways and Private Collections

The preservation movement in Nottingham was relatively slow to get off the ground. In the first two decades after the demise of steam, one had to journey to the GCR in Leicestershire or the Midland Railway Centre in Derbyshire to experience the sights and sounds of a bygone age. The only local display of artefacts relating to Nottingham and the railway age was to be found at the City Council's Industrial Museum at Wollaton Hall. Further afield, the National Railway Museum at York also had some relics from Nottingham displayed, but for a City that had once boasted so many railways, there was little left to show for it.

Above and Right : A little piece of the Great Northern Railway from Nottingham lives on in the National Railway Museum at York. The two armed shunting somersault signal that stands against the south buttress of the Great Hall once stood adjacent to the Goods Yard Box at London Road Low Level Station. It dated from the end of the Nineteenth Century and was the last surviving somersault signal in the area, remaining in use into the 1980s. The signal was removed to the National Collection by BR when the yard was closed. The vandalised remains of the signal box were dismantled by enthusiasts with the intention re-erecting it at Ruddington. When dismantled however, the timber was found to be in poor condition, so was sadly not kept. The remaining materials are thought to have been dispersed after a period in storage.

2.1 Wollaton Hall Industrial Museum

The Industrial Museum housed in the outbuildings of Wollaton Hall, to the west of the City, is owned and run by Nottingham City Council. The ambitious brief it sets itself is to conserve and present to the public a representation of the City's industrial past. Given its modest size, the museum fits a great deal in, with extensive displays relating to the products of Raleigh and the City's lace manufacturing industry. The museum is crowded with immaculately restored examples of locally made products and machine tools, and an annexe houses a collection of stationary engines. The centrepiece of this is the magnificently restored pumping engine recovered from the waterworks at Basford, but other exhibits include the winding engine from Thorneywood Brickworks (Chapter 1, p15) and a pair of Fowler traction engines that once worked at Stoke Bardolph Sewage Works.

The largest railway exhibit at Wollaton is this Private Owner 7-plank wagon, in the livery of Clifton Colliery. The pit finished production in the sixties, and had originally been sunk to pay off the local landowners debts.

All restoration work at the museum has been carried out by volunteers from The Arkwright Society, who look after the exhibits and are only too happy to talk to visitors about them.

Unfortunately occupying a stable block at a stately home leaves little room for exhibits, and relics of the railway age tend to be large. The museum does acknowledge the role that railways played in Nottingham's development, and some interesting artefacts are to be found here, including a 7 plank coal wagon from Clifton Colliery outside in the courtyard, and a number of signs and small artefacts.

One nameplate from 46251 'City of Nottingham' is to be seen at Wollaton, together with nameplates from GWR locomotives, 'Bulwell Hall' and appropriately 'Wollaton Hall'.

The exhibits at Wollaton also include a nameplate from one of Sir William Stanier's magnificent Pacifics, No 46251 'City of Nottingham'. The locomotive famously worked into Nottingham Victoria on a special train in May 1965. When British Railways withdrew it, they offered it to Nottingham City Council to preserve. Sadly the City declined the offer and kept only a nameplate. The engine itself was cut up for scrap and today a model of it is displayed alongside the nameplate. This may seem unbelievable now, but in the 1960's the local authority had other priorities, and what was seen as the recent past was not worth justifying the finance to conserve. One would hope that the present day custodians of our industrial heritage have rather more foresight.

For many years, this corner of the Industrial Museum was the only public display of artefacts from the City's lost railways, setting aside some relics of the GCR that reside in the museum at Loughborough Central Station.

2.2 London Road - A Scheme Too Far

In the mid 1980s, a group of local enthusiasts and businessmen decided to address the City's lack of a dedicated transport museum and arranged a short term lease of the derelict GNR London Road Low Level Station, close to the heart of the City. The objective was to create a working transport museum and relay a short section of line on which to run demonstration trains. A few vintage road vehicles were moved into the train shed, and some limited work was undertaken to improve the fabric of the building and make it secure. Sadly there was neither the support nor finance available to get this ambitious scheme off the ground, The location of the site, in a dense urban area, made it too valuable commercially to support a heritage operation, and vulnerable to the attentions of vandals. Sadly the sum of these problems was insurmountable, and the project was quietly laid to rest.

After a number of years of remaining empty with a seemingly uncertain future, the old station eventually found use as a fitness centre and has now been beautifully restored. It is a shame that trains will never again grace the elegant train shed, but at least T C Hines' masterpiece has survived for future generations to admire.

A Brush Type 4 (Class 47) draws a train into Ruddington Depot in the late 1970s. The remains of the station lie in the distance, and the view was taken from the footbridge that spanned the lines at the point that the MOD siding diverged. Appendix 3 contains a BR work study exercise, recording how these movements were worked at Ruddington.

Rob Hancock

The former GNR station at London Road is seen here in the mid 1980s. It was once surrounded by a clutter of lesser railway buildings, but these were demolished when BR vacated the site and passed it to the City Council. Today the station buildings have become a fitness centre, but they very nearly became a transport museum.

2.3 The Great Central is Reborn

Whilst attempts were being made to create the London Road museum, another transport heritage project was struggling to make the transition from pipe dream to reality. A group based at the Great Central Railway at Loughborough had been working hard for years to promote an extension north to Nottingham. This was to utilise the freight only section of remaining line that terminated at Ruddington. The closure of the MOD's Ordnance, Storage, Surplus and Disposals Depot (OSDD) here meant that the section of the former Great Central main line serving it, together with a large rail connected site comprising numerous generous storage buildings became available, and the project might be achievable.

The site had passed into local authority ownership, and Nottinghamshire County Council and Rushcliffe Borough Council were together looking at this time for how best to develop the 315 Acre site of the Ordnance Depot. In addition to industrial and employment sites, the development brief for the site earmarked a significant portion for leisure and recreation, including a country park, and the two Authorities agreed that the creation of a transport museum and railway preservation scheme was an attractive proposition, and sustainable use of the site. In 1989 the Great Central Railway Northern Development Association was set up, as a faction of the preservation group at Loughborough. Development of the new site was to be independent of the parent railway, and to facilitate this, the Great Central Railway (Nottingham) Ltd operating company was established.

Freight traffic continued to operate on the 5 mile section between Loughborough and the plasterboard works at Hotchley Hill, but the section of line from Rushcliffe Halt to Ruddington had passed into the hands of Rushcliffe Borough Council when BR operations ceased. This was subsequently leased to the fledgling preservation group. The first locomotive to arrive at the site was an ex North Eastern Y7 tank from Loughborough, and this ran on a number of open days. The state of the permanent way, earthworks and structures had deteriorated whilst the line had been out of use. Volunteers cleared much of the undergrowth and carried out repairs to earthworks, drainage systems and structures. Improvements were made to the trackwork, and a shrewd arrangement with rail maintenance companies to use the line as a training facility resulted in significant improvement to the permanent way.

Barnstone Tunnel in the late 1970s. Both tracks were still in situ at this time, but the route by now just served the MOD disposals depot at Ruddington. The gradient post marking the summit of the climb from Nottingham is visible.

Rob Hancock

The section of the old Ordnance Depot that formed the basis of the transport museum was to see significant change as the site developed. Many of the original buildings were demolished before the volunteers moved in, but several storage warehouses and most critically, the rail served workshop remained intact. Tracks were realigned and new ones laid. A new south facing chord was constructed between the depot and the main line, to create a triangular junction and allow the turning of locomotives. Work began on construction of a terminus station, and an impressive two road engine shed was erected, built in the classic Victorian style. A signal box was erected at the station throat, utilising the rescued upper storey of Neasden box, on a new brick base. Once fully commissioned, this will control departing passenger trains and access to and from the yard and shed. Work has gradually progressed, and by the summer of 2008, a new 700' platform had been virtually completed, to replace a temporary timber platform.

Plans for development of the railway extend beyond the old depot site at Ruddington. The group's long term ambition is to rebuild Ruddington Station in

its original style. The platform and Down line have survived in situ, although the adjoining goods yard succumbed to a housing development a few years ago.

Aside from owners of locomotives and rolling stock, other groups moving to the Heritage Centre, included the Nottingham Society of Model & Experimental Engineers, who built an extensive miniature railway around the site, a model railway group who have built GCR related model railway layouts, and vintage bus enthusiasts, whose fleet of locally connected vehicles has proved enormously popular at open days.

A number of unexpected challenges needed to be met by the preservation group, not least of which was a major landslip at Barnstone Tunnel in December 2006. A burst water main alongside the A6006 crossing the line went unnoticed for some time. The increase in pore water pressure of the soil and saturation of the cutting side slope eventually led to a slippage of approximately 150 tonnes. Fortunately the masonry of the tunnel barrel and the permanent way suffered little damage, but the disruption was enormous, a wing wall suffered damage, and the track and drainage became contaminated with clay slurry. It took a massive effort to coordinate the clear up, and was an unwelcome distraction for those endeavouring to reinstate and operate the line.

The line into Ruddington Depot is seen on the left in this 1984 view. The singled remains of the main line are to the right. The footbridge is known locally as 50 Steps, and has survived to form part of the preservation scheme.

The future for this venture is an exciting one. The vision driving it is the prospect of steam hauled passenger trains running from the southern fringe of Nottingham to the northern fringe of Leicester. The proposed extension of Nottingham's tram system (NET) south along the abandoned GC formation at Wilford offers a tantalising opportunity to bring visitors from the City by tram to the heritage railway, along a route once taken by the Master Cutler and the South Yorkshireman.

The opening of Leicester North station, close to the site of the old Belgrave & Birstall station has brought the overall vision a step nearer. Ways are now being sought to replace the long demolished bridge across the Midland Railway at Loughborough. Creation of a separate shed and yard to the east of the line will allow the formation to the north of Loughborough to be released for relaying track. Once the two sections are reconnected, and the stations on the northern section are completed, the result will be one of the longest preserved railways in the country, and the only double track main line in preservation.

Three photographs from the camera of Rob Hancock, recording the connection to Ruddington Depot in the late 1970s.

Above : Until 1974, Weekday Cross marked the northern extremity of the rail link to Ruddington. The formation was abandoned after a new connection to the Midland was built at Loughborough, and trains to Ruddington used the section to the south.

Top Right : From 1972 the headshunt at Weekday Cross shared the formation with the Nottingham District Heating mains, which provided the Victoria Centre with heat.

Bottom Right ; A pair of Class 25s set back through the overgrown platform with a fitted freight for Ruddington Depot. The train is reversing into the exchange sidings, having arrived via Loughborough. The trees in the background were planted when the line was built in 1899.

More pictures taken by Rob Hancock; these recording operations at Ruddington.

Top : 'Peaks' were employed on OSDD trains in the '70s/'80s. An unidentified loco sets back out of the Depot with an empty, before heading south down the old main line.

Above : 46002 stands in the down platform at the head of a fitted freight comprising mainly of vans and vehicle flats. This particular working was setting back into the Depot one day in February 1977 when it suffered the misfortune of a derailment.

Top : Toton Depot's steam crane was called out and a number of vehicles had to be righted to clear the line including a flat wagon carrying an unfortunate 1972 Austin Mini.

Above : The Mini eats ballast, as onlookers watch proceedings from Fifty Steps Bridge. The single Class 20 on Toton's breakdown train is visible beneath the bridge. The car carries the sign 'Disabled Driver-no hand signals'.

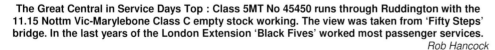

The Great Central in Service Days Top : Class 5MT No 45450 runs through Ruddington with the 11.15 Nottm Vic-Marylebone Class C empty stock working. The view was taken from 'Fifty Steps' bridge. In the last years of the London Extension 'Black Fives' worked most passenger services.

Rob Hancock

Above : Annesley 9F 92092 heads north with an unfitted freight. Ruddington, 1963. The empty working would have been destined for Annesley yard

Rob Hancock

Top : 8F No 48088 runs into Ruddington with a Down empty mineral working in the 1960s. Fifty Steps is visible in the background. The point rods in the foreground led to Ruddington Box, immediately behind the Photographer.

Rob Hancock

Above : Gresley V2 60847 'St Peters School York' approaches Ruddington with the final Sunday morning Marylebone-Nottm Vic semi-fast, in March 1963. The V2s were regular performers on the GCR in the 1950s, but after the route transferred to the LMR in 1958, LNER designs were less frequently seen.

Rob Hancock

Barnstone Tunnel in the 1960s : Four further views through the lens of Rob Hancock.

Top : An Up freight emerges into the daylight in charge of a Stanier 8F, possibly No 48035.

Above : A Marylebone-Nottm Vic working bursts from Barnstone Tunnel, headed by rebuilt Royal Scot No 46163 'Civil Service Rifleman' of Annesley Shed.

Top : Rebuilt Royal Scot No 46122 'Royal Ulster Rifleman' of Annesley Shed is seen about to enter the tunnel with the 17.15 Nottm Vic-Marylebone. Summer 1963.

Above : B1 61167 emerges into the sunlight with the 17.15 Nottm Vic-Marylebone service. B1 s were familiar locos on the line throughout the 1950s, but by the summer of 1963, when this view was recorded, they were starting to become scarce.

Into the Preservation Era

The Ruddington Depot site has now become the Nottingham Transport Heritage Centre, and headquarters of efforts to bring life back to this section of the old Great Central main line. The following selection of views record the progress that had been made at Ruddington by the summer of 2008.

Below : A Ruston diesel-mechanical shunting loco (BR Class 05) stands outside the newly completed two road engine shed. The shed provides welcome shelter to a number of the centre's assets, including GCR Barnum coaching stock and the English Electric Type 3 (BR Class 37) visible in the right hand road. Reclaimed period windows built into the shed add to its authentic appearance.

Top Right : The operating floor section of Neasden Signal box has undergone transformation, since its recovery by the group. Today it sits on a new brick base at the end of the new station platform, and it will eventually control train movements both in the station, and the adjacent yard. The lamp room is a faithful replica of a feature once common on the railway, and now all but extinct.

Bottom Right : The new station platform was nearing completion when photographed. The track will be laid after it is finished, and one day it will hopefully be the departure point for trains to Leicester North.

44

Top : D2959 (BR Class 04) is just one of a variety of locomotives stood outside the old Depot maintenance shed. A number of original MOD buildings have found new uses on the site.

Above : The 45 Ton steam crane is a popular exhibit. It has been operated at a number of public events, and has proved a useful asset. The design is similar, but slightly larger than the crane illustrated on page 56 attending a derailment at Ruddington in the 1970s.

Top : The yard is presently crowded with restoration projects. The well wagon seen here is an MOD design for carrying tanks and other heavy military equipment. Doubtless many visited the site during its days as an MOD depot. This one carries a boiler that awaits restoration.

Above : Ruddington is a home for vintage and retired buses as well as railway stock. The venue is host to several popular events featuring preserved buses and other vintage transport.

Above : An English Electric Type 3 (Class 37) approaches the end of an overhaul in the new loco shed at Ruddington. Covered facilities such as this are essential for major works to locomotives and rolling stock.

Top Right: The raised 3½" & 5" gauge tracks of the Nottingham Society of Model & Experimental Engineers seen, together with the signal cabin that controls the miniature signals. This was built by a society member and based on a GCR ground cabin design.

Bottom Right : A view of the departure road from the heritage centre site. The footbridge connects with the Country Park, developed on part of the former MOD site.

A fine example of an LNER bracket Starter frames this view of Ruddington's signal box. Lattice post signals were common on the LNER, but are seldom seen in the preservation world.

Further south on the main line, the remains of the Down Starter colour light signal are seen at Rushcliffe Halt. The diamond denotes track circuiting to be in use. This safety system detects vehicles in the track section, by passing an electric current between the two rails, via the wheels and axles of the engine or rolling stock. An instrument in the section box registers the flow of current, and hence the presence of the train. Although the signal dates from the 1950s, this method of train detection was in operation right from the line's original opening in 1899.

2.4 The Midland Railway Trust

Although situated in Derbyshire, The Midland Railway Trust at Butterley is worthy of brief inclusion since it includes a number of exhibits that originated in or around Nottingham. The Trust moved to Butterley in 1973, and started by recreating the station there, meticulously re-erecting buildings from Whitwell, on the Mansfield- Worksop line.

As the site developed, other buildings were moved to nearby Swanwick Junction, and these eventually included the main erecting shed from William Rigley's wagon works on Bulwell Common, and Linby Station Signal Box. The former houses a collection of preserved stock, including a fireless engine from the Boots Company at Beeston and a crane engine from Stanton & Staveley (see Chapter 1). Several signal box nameboards with Nottinghamshire connections also reside there.

The Linby Station signal box has been attractively restored and erected on a sturdy, although non-original brick base. Fully equipped, this demonstration box is open to the public.

Linby Signal Box is seen above at its new home at Swanwick Junction, and below as it was in the early 1980s, boarded up and out of use at its original location. The Midland Railway Centre is home to numerous retired Midland signal boxes, and well worth a visit for anyone with an interest in mechanical signalling.

The Midland Railway Centre's immaculate 3F No 16410 has a clear signal for departure from Butterley Station, with a train of vintage stock in August 2008. Little remained here when the Trust arrived in 1973 but thanks to the efforts of volunteers, today Butterley Station looks much as it did in the 1920s.

2.5 Private Collections

In addition to memorabilia and relics preserved in public museums and visitor centres, a surprising amount of items have survived in private ownership. Enamelled railway signs in particular have become hugely collectible and today command large sums of money. British Railways recognised the demand in the late 1960s, and many redundant signs were dispatched to Collectors' Corner at Euston, for sale. Those that didn't go to Euston were unofficially removed by railway employees and over zealous enthusiasts.

Items of signalling interest picked up by the Author over the years. All have connections with Nottingham area boxes or locations, and many came from specialist auctions or Collector's fairs. In recent times the Internet has transformed collecting, and much of what could once be found at car boot sales for reasonable sums now appear on the likes of Ebay at inflated prices. Despite this, it is still possible to find the occasional bargain. The LNER Welch Patent signal lamp at the back originally came from the GNR Derbyshire Extension. It still works, and cost the modest sum of £5 from an antiques fair.

It is reasonable to say that virtually every totem and running in board from all of the City's stations that were in public use in the 1960s probably still survive in collections around the country. One or two are on public display at places like the City's Industrial Museum and at Ruddington, but the majority adorn the walls of private collectors.

Interest in 'railwayana' can extend to old documents. The page above is an extract from Mackenzie & Holland's 1913 tender to the Great Northern Railway for resignalling in the Nottingham area. Although the shunting signal pictured on page 36 at the start of the Chapter was not part of this contract, other signals in the London Road yard were. It can be seen from this document that the new cost of a twin arm somersault like the one in York Museum was £30 10s. The layout of this Bill of Quantities is similar to ones used in construction today.

Station signs and locomotive nameplates command considerable sums of money, and only occasionally come onto the market, but many items of lesser value, but arguably equal interest or with local connections can still be picked up if one knows where to shop. A visit to a collector's swapmeet such as those held at the GCR or a specialist auction can leave one wondering whether anything discarded by the railway was actually scrapped. Interest in memorabilia now seems to extend to every aspect of railway life, and collectors specialise in tickets, oil lamps, depot pay checks, timetables and handbills, signal box instruments and even crockery and silverware. The motivating factor for many older collectors is simply nostalgia, and the desire to own part of a now lost way of life. The fascination appears to have infected a fresh generation though, who can have no memories of steam traction or the pre-Beeching railway network. Today demand for all things railway continues unabated, and what was once viewed by many as a harmless hobby practiced by eccentric rail enthusiasts has become a respectable investment industry.

Whatever the motivation may be for collecting and conserving these bygones, one might conclude that interest in our lost railway lines, and transport in what was arguably a more civilised age seems set continue well into the future. If this is so then perhaps it can be no bad thing.

Above : Nottinghamshire signal box name boards on public display in the Midland Railway Trust's museum building at Swanwick in Derbyshire. The upper boards are of Midland origin, whilst Basford Sidings was an LMS box, and appears in Volume 2 on p45. The Pye Hill board is from a Great Northern box once situated on the branch to Pinxton. Museums such as those at Butterley, Loughborough and Ruddington are frequently reliant on loans from private collections to furnish their displays.

Above : A selection of Great Northern and LNER signal box nameboards from the Nottingham area, in the collection of a local enthusiast in 2009. Name boards were invariably removed from signal boxes before demolition. Most still survive in private collections, and despite their unwieldy size, and often crude finish, they are highly sought after.

Right : A nameplate and builders plate from Gedling Colliery's Barclay shunter that once worked the landsale wharf at Mapperley. These two plates form part of the same collection as the boards above. This photograph makes an interesting comparison with those on pages 11 and 12, showing the plates on the engine in the 1950s.

A selection of surviving name boards from Nottingham stations. Large enamelled signs like these are bulky and by necessity often have to be stored outside, leading to gradual deterioration. The top three boards appear in photographs at their original locations, in Volumes 1 and 2. The cast iron seat sign below is on the wall of the museum at Loughborough Central.

This LNER milepost appears on page 61, abandoned in the old GCR tunnel under Thurland Street It was found by the author during a site inspection in 2005. Subsequently restored, it now resides in a corner of his study; a memento of a more unusual day at the office.

3.0 Hidden Heritage

3.1 Manvers Street L&NWR

Freight, Bananas & Kitchen Surplus.

Of the pre-grouping companies operating in Nottingham, the London & North Western Railway probably had the smallest market share. It had running rights over the Great Northern Railway from Saxondale Junction, near Bingham, and joint ownership of a number of lines through the Vale of Belvoir. It also operated yard facilities at Colwick, together with an eight road engine shed there. Until the 1880s however it had no independent facility in Nottingham itself, and shared the Great Northern's London Road passenger terminus. Goods facilities were catered for by means of a single storey shed, leased from the GN.

Passenger operations in Nottingham were never likely to amount to more than a provincial operation for "The Premier Line". Lying too far east of the Company's main sphere of operations, it was reached by indirect secondary routes. Euston saw freight operations differently though. Nottingham was a growing city on the edge of a large coalfield, with well developed textile and manufacturing industries, and a growing population that needed to be serviced.

The yard at Colwick gained access to lucrative coal traffic, but facilities would be needed in the City itself, if a larger market was to be reached.

In 1887 the Company obtained Parliamentary Powers and started building what would be its only independent line in the County of Nottinghamshire. Opened the following year, and at a mere 20 chains in length, it was the shortest distinct line on the Company's books. It left the Great Northern at Trent Lane Junction, and four tracks climbed away to the north at a gradient of 1 in 102, to terminate on a bluff of high land behind Sneinton Hermitage.

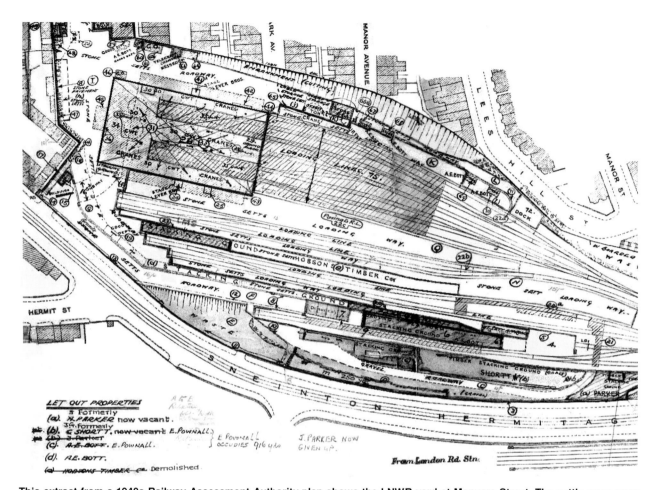

This extract from a 1940s Railway Assessment Authority plan shows the LNWR yard at Manvers Street. The cattle pens were out of use by this time (denoted as storage racks). The main building was severely damaged by bombing during the war, but the plan is based on pre-war mapping, so shows the warehouse largely as built.

Here, a compact elevated yard was built, together with a substantial three storey goods warehouse. A small signal box controlled entry and exit to the yard. The soft sandstone under the building was excavated away, and the entire lower storey was built beneath ground.

Access was taken via a short cut and cover tunnel from Manvers Street. Freight vehicles entered the structure at effectively first floor level, on four tracks, supported by wrought iron beams and red brick jack arches. Iron columns supported the upper floor, and the roof was supported by iron trusses. A total of eight freight hoists connected all three floors, and the offices were incorporated into the western end of the ground floor. Road vehicles approached the rail level part of the depot from Newark Street, and livestock was driven from the pens on the south side of the yard, down the ramp to Manvers Street and through the streets of Sneinton to the markets on Meadow Lane.

One can assume the Company made a reasonable return on its investment because freight traffic remained busy through the early part of the Twentieth Century. Additional traffic continued to be handled at the neighbouring GNR yard, and passenger services continued to use London Road (Low Level). In LMS days, the site offered access to the bustling east of the City, that other facilities, like the Midland Railway's Wilford Road Depot were less well positioned to exploit. Livestock traffic had ceased by this time, to be replaced by timber traffic, and the pens were used as stackyards. Use of the site was dramatically interrupted on the evening of May 17th, 1941, when the depot was wrecked by an air raid. Timber in the adjacent stackyard caught fire and the goods shed was left a burned out shell. The roof and large elements of the exterior walls were destroyed, and bombs penetrated to rail level, exploding, and collapsing sections of platform into the undercroft below.

The site was cleared, and damage made good where possible. The underground warehousing was spared the wholesale destruction of the upper storeys, and continued in use, but in the post-war years of austerity, no capital was available to invest in the site.

The brick and wrought iron vaulting beneath the platforms in the warehouse is shown in this view. Riveted iron cross beams carry the load, and the brickwork above these raises the level, to create the platform. The arch work reduces weight further, and the platform surface is carried by intermediate jack arches. The arches springing from the bottom flanges of the main beams in the top right of the picture carry the permanent way (see cross section overleaf).

The entrance to the underground portion of the LNWR warehouse on Manvers Street is seen, together with the base of the ramp to yard level in June 2007. No trace of the railway now exists at the upper level.

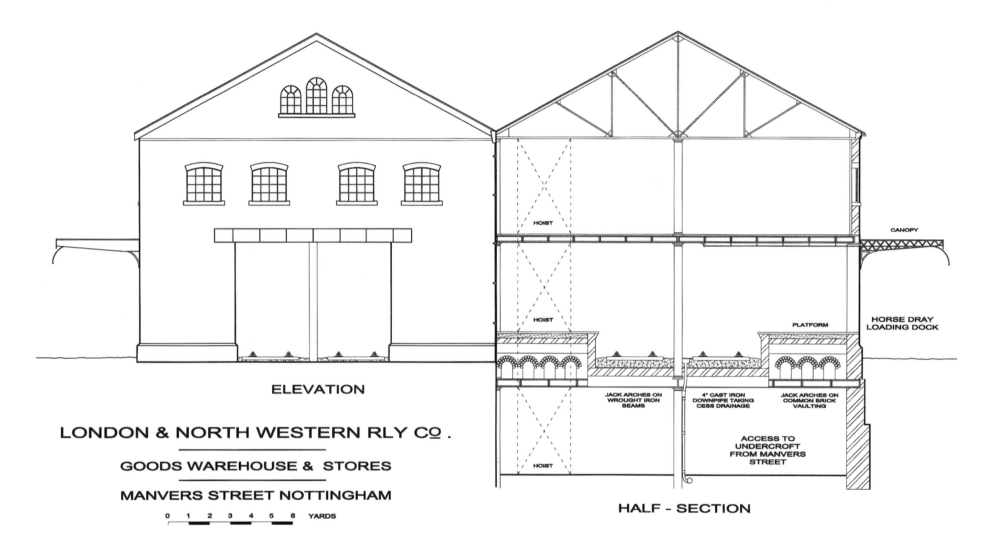

ELEVATION

LONDON & NORTH WESTERN RLY C⁰.

GOODS WAREHOUSE & STORES

MANVERS STREET NOTTINGHAM

0 1 2 3 4 5 6   YARDS

HALF - SECTION

Labels within the section:

HOIST

HOIST

HOIST

CANOPY

HORSE DRAY LOADING DOCK

PLATFORM

JACK ARCHES ON WROUGHT IRON BEAMS

4" CAST IRON DOWNPIPE TAKING CESS DRAINAGE

JACK ARCHES ON COMMON BRICK VAULTING

ACCESS TO UNDERCROFT FROM MANVERS STREET

Manvers Street Goods Depot was the only major piece of infrastructure built in the City by the LNWR. The three storey structure was finished in red brick, and rail traffic entered by means of four tracks at effectively first floor level. The structural supports were wrought iron throughout, and tens of thousands of rivets held the huge number of component parts together. The building incorporated no less than 15 hand operated 30CWT cranes at platform level, and these were supplemented by eight goods lifts, and a 5 Ton crane in the yard just outside. Overhead tracking above each of the six loading bays may have been part of a hoist system. The author has uncovered contemporary plans of floor layouts for the structure, but elevations and photographs that predate the bombing seem to be rare. This end elevation was prepared by the author, based on measurements of surviving below ground elements, dimensions taken from railway land plans, a photograph of the bomb damaged structure, and in the case of the roof truss, a certain amount of educated guesswork based on contemporary practice in similar structures.

With general merchandise traffic in retreat on the railway, the underground warehouse was eventually leased to Fyffes, who found the cool temperatures ideal for the storage of fruit, and in particular bananas.

Railway use came to an end on the site in June 1966, and the cleared yard area passed to Nottingham City Council. In the following decade, a housing estate sprang up on the site of the sidings, although care was taken not to build over the remaining underground portion of the old warehouse. The embankment of the connecting line was removed, along with the bridges over Sneinton Hermitage and Meadow Lane, and the site was taken over by a local scrap metal merchant that had previously leased part of the yard.

Barely a quarter of the undercroft is recorded here. The structure was built on a truly impressive scale, and what remains of it has survived in remarkably good condition. Little corrosion is evident in the ironwork and the brickwork is generally dry and defect free. The present use of the site is evident from this view, and the author is indebted to the Site Manager for allowing the pictures to be taken.

The retaining walls bounding the site of the yard still remained, and the ramp once used by cattle became a public footpath. By the base of this, the old portal leading to the underground warehouse also survived, but to the casual observer there was little else left. Hidden from site, the underground warehouse continued in use, finding different occupiers as the years progressed. In its retirement years it has found a use as a sales outlet for surplus catering equipment, and it looks likely to continue in that use for the foreseeable future.

The granite sett paved roadway into the underground portion of the warehouse is seen here in 2007. The wrought iron beams forming the roof of the approach are set out in a fan arrangement to follow the curved profile of the tunnel. Aside from the road traffic, this view can have little changed in 120 years. This approach road leads into an elevated loading dock, where goods were transferred to the backs of horse drawn delivery drays.

3.2 Other Subterranean Survivors

The Great Central Railway

40 years ago Nottingham Victoria closed its doors for the last time, and the bulldozers moved in. The buildings were quickly demolished, to be replaced by a shopping centre, bus station and multi-storey car park. Two freight lines remained in situ until May 1968, when the final freight movements on this portion of the GC were diverted away. A single track headshunt from Weekday Cross remained in Thurland Street Tunnel until 1974, when this too was lifted. When the Victoria Centre opened in 1971, the only obvious clues to the former station's existence were the clock tower and the north cutting with the remaining boarded up Mansfield Road tunnel entrance.

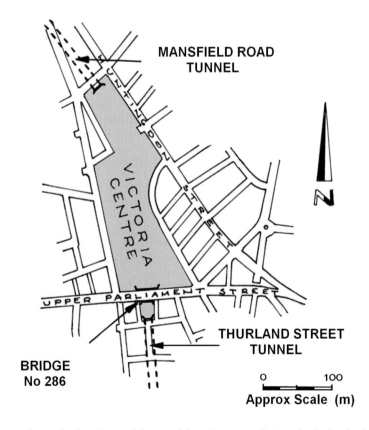

MANSFIELD ROAD TUNNEL

VICTORIA CENTRE

UPPER PARLIAMENT STREET

THURLAND STREET TUNNEL

BRIDGE No 286

0   100

Approx Scale (m)

The sketch above shows the locations of the surviving structures that are looked at in detail. All are inaccessible to the public, and in the case of Thurland Street Tunnel and Parliament Street Bridge, the majority of the City's inhabitants have little idea that they exist, or that a mighty railway station once stood where shoppers now browse.

A pair of Thompson Class 01s restart a southbound coal working by Parliament Street bridge in 1958. The footbridge to the north of the road bridge would be demolished a few years later, to facilitate the building of a store for Boots, on an extension of the bridge. This new structure was demolished in 1967/8.

C A Hill (Courtesy J Bull)

In the late 'nineties the north cutting was redeveloped and, save the boarded up portal of Mansfield Road Tunnel, little now appears to be left. Hidden away beneath the bustling City however, lie less apparent reminders of the last main line of the classic era.

From time to time, Engineers from the Highway Authority are required to inspect structures or voids beneath the public highway. Working for the City of Nottingham has over the years allowed the author a privileged glimpse into some of these hidden places.

Parliament Street Bridge was built of steel. Its trapezoidal single span deck varied in span 76 feet to 130 feet, as it crossed the converging lines at the south end of the station. This substantial bridge incorporated service tunnels beneath the footpaths, and its steel parapets were disguised with a red brick curtain wall on the road side. An access was built through the north parapet, with a distribution bridge and steps providing public access to the southern extremity of the two main island platforms. The design of these steps was similar to those used at smaller single island platform stations elsewhere on the line.

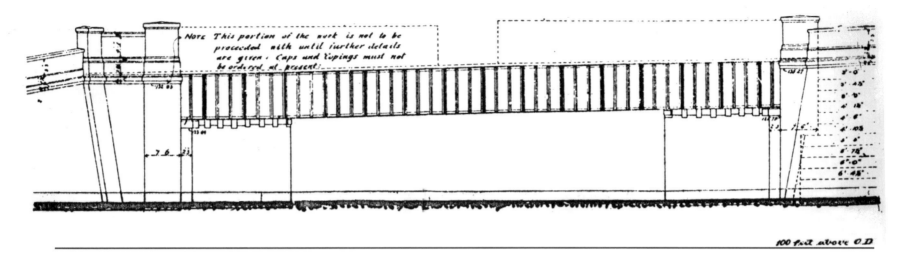

Note This portion of the work is not to be proceeded with until further details are given. Caps and Copings must not be ordered at present.

100 feet above O.D.

Bridge No 286 was constructed with very substantial (10' deep) steel beams. These were required to carry the load of the public highway over the maximum span distance of 130'. This northern elevation dates from before the parapet design was finalised. The gap in the parapet accommodated the south entrance, which led to a distribution footbridge connecting with platforms six and seven. The carriageway side of the parapet was brick faced, although the main construction was in plate steel, similar to the main beams. Today the deck, abutments and wing walls survive, hidden from the view of the general public in an underground car park.

Plan Courtesy Nottingham City Council

A main beam is seen here, together with a section of cross-bracing that was added to the bridge in later life. The photograph was taken during an inspection in February 2001. This bridge underwent strengthening in 2008.

Nottingham City Council

A B1 (possibly 61067 'Ourebi') heads an Up loaded coal working out of Nottingham Victoria on a late summer evening in 1965. The short lived steel trestle extension to Bridge No 286 that carried Boot's store can be seen to good effect in this unusual view.

Rob Hancock

After closure, and demolition of Nottingham Victoria, Bridge No 286 was hidden away from public gaze, and forgotten by many. The parapets were removed, and it was hemmed in by shop fronts. The bridge over the railway site (now an underground car park) survived virtually intact however, and today it continues to carry heavy traffic and thousands of pedestrians. Shrouded in pigeon netting, the superstructure is only visible from inside the car park. It is from here that the outlines of the massive retaining walls and Union Road bridge abutments can also be seen. Within the deck, the original access tunnels continue to be used by a variety of service cables and pipes.

The underground car park extends south into the cutting beyond Parliament Street Bridge, and it finishes at a breeze block wall with a small door in it.

Beyond the locked door is a void extending the full height of the old cutting, dominated by the intact portal of Thurland Street Tunnel, with its distinctive curved wing-walls still in place. Unfortunately the date stone above the crown is no longer visible, but much remains as it had been in railway days. The tunnel has been used to route pipes for the District Heating System since 1973, but the site of the down line remains clear, and the original ballast is still in place. A few sleepers, oddments of rusting signalling equipment and other items of interest including a milepost and gradient post were still in the tunnel in 2005. Cable support brackets and signal pulleys (some with wires still connected) were attached to the down abutment. The most surprising piece of remaining infrastructure was a treadle operated clapper that would have warned trains using the final head-shunt that the buffer stops were close.

The 392 yard long tunnel was partly constructed by cut and cover, and partly by heading. The roof comprises Staffordshire Brindled bricks, and the height of this steps down near the end of Thurland Street, possibly denoting the transition from heading to cut and cover. With the exception of the extremities, by the portals, the abutment walls are generally formed in the natural sandstone, through which the tunnel was cut. Refuges are hewn out of this at intervals, headed by blue brick arches. These are now mostly crammed with construction rubble, or rubbish associated with vagrants sleeping rough, which was a problem here before erection of a steel grille across the south portal in the 1980s.

The south portal at Weekday Cross formed a backdrop to many photographs taken during operational days, and continued to be a local landmark for three decades after the railway was abandoned. Sadly it has now been blocked off by construction of Nottingham's new Contemporary Arts Centre across the formation, and is no longer visible.

Right : The scale of the structure can be gauged from the size of the access platform, and its two occupants. Low level lighting and anti-pigeon netting make the bridge difficult to see, and the black paint coating the steelwork does little to help.

Nottingham City Council

At the south end of Victoria Centre car park is a locked doorway. Stepping through it leads to a hidden realm. The portal beyond leads to Thurland Street Tunnel, and is made all the more impressive by virtue of the confined space it occupies. Standing in this massive gateway to a pitch black abyss is fascinating and perhaps just a little unsettling.

The flash of the camera picks out the lime mortar pointing of the arch barrel, and the mottled sandstone of the abutments. The pipes are steam mains for the District Heating System.

The scale of the tunnel portal is virtually impossible to convey in a photograph, even when taken with a 28mm wide angle lens.

Below : Tucked against the down line abutment is a timber post carrying the remains of a signal. The aspect and lamp have gone, but brackets and the counterbalance weight are still in place. Its operating wire stretches away to the long demolished Victoria South Box, supported by a line of pulleys set in the sandstone. This was almost certainly No 68 in the South box, an elevated shunting signal for movements at the south of the station.

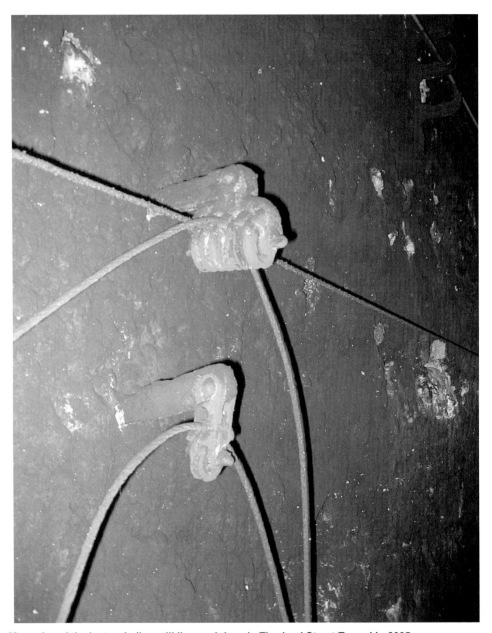

Memories of the last main line still lingered deep in Thurland Street Tunnel in 2005.

Above : Severed signal wires hang from their pulleys on the down side of the tunnel. One still stretches tantalisingly in the direction of the long vanished Victoria South box.

Left : A treadle operated clapper lies in the cess. This once sounded a warning to trains approaching the end of the head-shunt that existed in the tunnel between 1968 and 1974.

Above : The southern end of Thurland Street Tunnel is seen here on the last day of main line operation on 3rd September 1966. Merchant Navy Class Pacific 35030 Elder Dempster Lines makes a dramatic sight as it heads the southbound leg of the Great Central Railtour, organised by the LCGB. Bullied Pacifics were occasional visitors to the London Extension, but this was the only time a rebuilt locomotive worked the line during BR days. Southern Region coaching stock also appeared regularly on the Bournemouth-York express, right up to the final years of operation.

Rob Hancock

Top Left : In 2005, a gradient post stands tucked against the down abutment. The metal numerals have long gone, but their impression is just about legible.

Bottom Left : An LNER intermediate milepost lies abandoned in the Up formation, uprooted in 1973 to make way for heating pipes of the District Heating System, which are just visible.

The south portal of Thurland Street Tunnel and associated retaining walls are seen here in 1982. This was the point where the Grantham line branched away from the Great Central's main line. The pipes on the right side of the formation carry steam, generated at Eastcroft Refuse Incinerator. These heat the Victoria Centre, which was built on the site of the old station. This area was built over in 2007/8, and both entrances to the tunnel are now hidden from view.

Victoria Station was also accessed by tunnel to the north. Mansfield Road Tunnel measured 1189 yards in length, and was constructed on a rising gradient of 1 in 132. It emerged at Carrington Station, before the line again plunged below ground. The disused south portal is still visible beyond the shopping centre's car park, but the northern end at Carrington Station was filled over in the late 1980s.

Unlike Thurland Street, Mansfield Road Tunnel was constructed entirely by heading. The first ten yards are brick lined, but the remainder again has natural sandstone abutments. The tunnel is built on a reverse curve, so virtually no daylight penetrated the centre portion, even before the ends were blocked. Refuges of similar design were again cut into the sandstone, and substantial chambers were excavated out of the rock on each side, approximately mid way through, presumably for maintenance personnel.

When the tunnel was inspected in 2002, it was still littered with reminders of its railway past. Bullhead track keys and smashed batteries littered the trackbed, and

the timber cable conduit remained in place on the Up side. Two sleepers, complete with chairs represented the last vestige of the Up line, about 500 yards from the south portal. Other recognisable relics included a signal post set into the Down abutment at the southern end, an S&T trackside cabinet and strangely, pieces of wagon brake gear. A broken gradient post stands by the north portal. The tunnel mouth itself is sealed off with a mass concrete wall. Steps up the wall lead to the base of an inspection chamber, the shaft of which surfaces in an access road, serving a development on the site of Carrington Station.

Jubilee No 45643 'Rodney' draws past Victoria North Signal Box, and approaches Mansfield Road Tunnel with a Summer Saturday Poole-Bradford train. LMS locomotive types dominated passenger services in the final years of the London Extension, although this locomotive is likely to have originated from Farnley Junction shed.

Rob Hancock

To the north of Carrington Station lay the Great Central's third tunnel in the City. After closure, the interior of Sherwood Rise Tunnel was used by British Telecom as a storage facility for some years, with its ends bricked up. It was abandoned in around 1980, and the southern end of the tunnel was buried when the Carrington Station site was redeveloped. The northern portal has been buried more recently, almost to its crown level. The interior void remains, but no safe access is presently available (even for official inspection purposes).

Colwick K3 No 61982 pulls out of the north facing bay of Platform 5, and heads for the gloomy and smoke filled depths of Mansfield Road Tunnel early in 1958. This local service would probably have been destined for Derby Friargate, via Bagthorpe Junction and the Great Northern Railway's Derbyshire Extension.

C A Hill (Courtesy J Bull)

PLATE 2.

Fig. II.

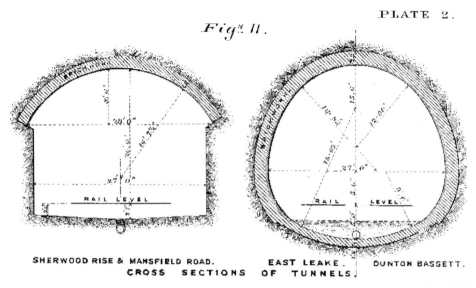

SHERWOOD RISE & MANSFIELD ROAD.　EAST LEAKE.　DUNTON BASSETT.
CROSS SECTIONS OF TUNNELS

The Great Central tunnels will probably be destined to continue to lie undisturbed indefinitely, save the occasional visit by Local Authority Engineers. They no longer provide routes anywhere, and being blocked off without through ventilation, they are classified as confined spaces and potentially susceptible to the build up of toxic gases. Consequently they are only entered by qualified personnel with breathing apparatus, and they are kept securely closed, to prevent the curious, or the homeless from straying inside.

Whilst it is sad to see these well constructed assets lying abandoned, consolation can be taken from the thought that perhaps centuries from now they will continue to exist, together with their scattering of steam age relics, long after any above ground trace of the disused route has gone.

Left : Extracts from contemporary GCR Construction plans showing the general arrangement of tunnel bores on the line. The left section is representative of Sherwood Rise, Mansfield Road and Thurland Street Tunnels, where the tunnels were constructed through stable rock formations. The right section is representative of the short tunnel on the preserved section of the GC at Barnstone (see Chapter 2).

Below : The last original sleepers and chairs to remain in place on the Great Central, within the City of Nottingham. These are midway through Mansfield Road Tunnel, on the Up side. An elm bullhead key lies by the chair, where it was knocked out by rail recovery crews when the line was lifted in the summer of 1968. The timber artefacts in the tunnel show no signs of decay, and if left undisturbed, will probably be there in several hundred years time.

On a frosty morning in January 2002, a team of Engineers from Nottingham City Council prepare to carry out a structural inspection of the now boarded up Mansfield Road Tunnel.

The picture above shows the mass concrete wall sealing the northern end of Mansfield Road tunnel. A steel ladder climbs the wall, to an access manhole above. The white staining is a salt deposit, formed by water seeping through the wall. Construction debris litters the foreground.

The Great Northern Railway

The area to the north east of Nottingham's centre is notably undulating and those railway companies crossing it found it necessary to build a number of tunnels. The Great Northern had five in the area (excluding the burrowing junction at Bagthorpe). Four of these tunnels were to be found on a line that was barely four miles in length.

The Nottingham Suburban Railway was an independent concern that was operated by the Great Northern Railway from its opening in 1888. Passenger services finished as early as 1916, and through freight traffic finished when the line was damaged by bombs in 1941. The truncated line lingered on, serving brickworks at Mapperley and Porchester from Daybrook Junction until 1954, when it closed completely. Redevelopment progressively claimed virtually all of the formation. Porchester and Sherwood tunnels were buried in the 1960s and 1970s, but two tunnels survived into more recent times.

Ashwell's tunnel, beneath the old coach road to Woodthorpe Grange lasted until the early 1980s as a feature in Woodthorpe Park, and Sneinton Tunnel (also referred to as Bluebell Hill Tunnel) is, at the time of writing, the last survivor.

By 1979 the entrance to Sneinton Tunnel was looking decidedly sorry for itself. The copings had gone, the entrance had been partially filled in, and the mesh security fence had become overgrown. The City Council has done much to improve the condition of the structure in recent years, with the brickwork being repaired, and the parapet replaced in a style sympathetic to the original design.

Sneinton Tunnel found new use as a shooting range. It is seen here in 1989. The floodlighting is reflected by areas of clean engineering brick. Soot still encrusts some of the brickwork in the arch barrel.

The latter tunnel has found used for many years now as a shooting range, with a blockwork wall across the north portal, and the south portal buried. Powerful lights at the north end illuminate the depths of the void, and the workman's refuges built into the blue brick lining have been bricked up to prevent ricochets. Tightening up of gun laws and changing attitudes towards gun ownership has led to a decline in target shooting as a sport (although gun crime continues to increase). Locally, the number of small bore target ranges has declined over the past few years. How much longer Sneinton Tunnel will continue in this use remains to be seen.

The fifth tunnel on the Great Northern's Nottingham lines was the longest, and deepest. Mapperley Tunnel, on the 1875 Derbyshire Extension was 1132 yards long, and passed beneath the ridge of high ground passing to Mapperley Plains. The bore was brick lined for its full length, and the massive portals were faced with blue engineering bricks, and topped by gritstone cappings.

It was abandoned in 1960, and the western end filled in a few years later. The eastern end of the tunnel was left however, and the portal, together with the very overgrown and waterlogged approach cutting now lie abandoned amidst farmland.

By 1987 when the Author investigated the condition of the lining, little railway infrastructure was left in place. The brickwork had deteriorated significantly by the entrance, and the parapet had been pushed off into the cutting below.

Over the years there have been various plans for the site, including a planning application made at one stage by the County Council to use it as a tip for waste road surfacing materials. Whilst these plans came to nothing, it seems likely that the tunnel entrance will eventually be filled over. The surrounding farmland is now destined to be redeveloped for housing, as the City's urban sprawl migrates outwards. The old railway corridor is safeguarded as a tract of green space, but with residential developments in close proximity, it is unlikely that the deep cutting or crumbling tunnel entrance will be left accessible. The remaining ventilation shafts lie under the line of a projected new road, so it seems that time is about to finally run out.

Top Left : Mapperley Tunnel cut through a ridge of marl to a depth of approximately 200 feet, making it one of the deepest tunnels in the East Midlands. It suffered the effects of mining subsidence during much of its life, partially collapsing in 1923. Structural instability of the tunnel was the ultimate reason for the closure of the line in 1960. The severance of Colwick Yard from the Leen Valley coal traffic led indirectly to the closure of yard facility too. The crumbling east portal is seen here in 1980.

Bottom Left : 600m of the eastern end of the bore of Mapperley Tunnel is still open at the time of writing, but sited on private land, and the poor condition of the structure make exploring it inadvisable. This view from inside the portal dates from 1992, and the serious deterioration of the brick lining is apparent. The timber props in the crown of the arch were inserted by British Railways engineers in the late 1950s, and extensively fire damaged in the 1990s.

This slightly grainy view shows a refuge in the eastern side wall of Mapperley Tunnel, a short distance from the portal. The original brickwork has been renewed here, together with an adjoining section of lining. It is probable that this repair work was carried out after the 1923 collapse of a section of the structure, following ground movement.

3.3 Relics of the Midland Railway

Although most of the Midland Railway's Nottingham network survives, a great deal of associated infrastructure has been lost. No trace remains of the locomotive depot, or the substantial yards that lay to the west of Midland Station. Similarly, many original buildings have now long gone on the local routes. There are however, odd survivors tucked away in unexpected places.

Nuthall Road Crossing Keeper's Cottage

Hidden away at the back of an industrial yard in Radford lies the last original building associated with the Midland Railway's Leen Valley line. Rationalisation, cessation of passenger services, mothballing, reopening and realignment work has seen virtually all of the original structures demolished.

The Italianate-style Crossing Keeper's cottage dates from the mid nineteenth century, and was rendered largely redundant after the crossing it served was supplanted by Bobbers Mill Bridge in the 1930s. The crossing was stopped up altogether in the 1960s, and the cottage sold out of railway ownership. Today the crossing cottage is a derelict shell, missing much of its roof. Without any form of planning protection its long term survival prospects are bleak.

Carrington Street Goods Station

After the relocation of the Midland Railway station to Station Street in 1848, the site of the original Midland Counties Railway Station on Carrington Street was rebuilt as a goods depot. A wrought iron framed structure with a northlight roof was erected on the site of the old station, and for more than a century, the goods shed, fronted by an elegant Georgian style office building, was the most centrally located goods facility in the City.

The gradual run down of freight on the railways through the 1960s saw the old Midland facilities on Carrington Street, and those further to the west, on Wilford Road, slide into terminal decline. The last lines were lifted in the early 1980s, and the sites were sold out of railway ownership. The Carrington Street site was redeveloped and the City's new Magistrates Court sprang up on the site. Most of the railway infrastructure disappeared, but tucked away behind the old offices, the wrought iron structure of the old warehouse was given a new lease of life. The timber cladding of the south wall was replaced by a brick curtain wall, the roof glazing was renewed, and a multi level car park was built into the old structure, serving the Courts.

The two northernmost spans of Carrington Street railway bridge abut the warehouse, and one of these carried goods lines into the undercroft beneath Midland Station. These also became part of the Court facilities, housing workshops and stores. From Carrington Street there is little indication, other than the now listed office block, of surviving infrastructure. The car park is not publicly accessible, but the author was granted access, during an engineering inspection associated with works to the adjacent bridge.

The car park to the rear of the Magistrates Court is not all that it seems. The modern brick shell and lightweight rood cladding belie its much earlier underpinnings. The internal structure dates to 1868, and represents the last vestige of the Midland Railway's once extensive goods facilities in Nottingham.

Arthur Stocks

The white gables of the old Midland warehouse are visible above the roof of the Peak in this 1970s view. This building has found new life as a private car park.

Rob Hancock

A massive wrought iron lintel spanning one of the four original entrances to the shed is seen from inside the car park in October 2007. Elements of brickwork from the western outer wall also survive.

Substantial beams are supported by slender columns, to create a large open space inside. The car park structure is built into the frame of the old goods shed, but is independently supported and the original ironwork remains intact.

The plain brick to the side of the Goods Offices on Carrington Street is shown here. Today it is used as a store by the City's Magistrates Court. The buildings underwent major refurbishment at the same time as the transformation of the goods shed.

3.4 Tramway Traces

Almost certainly the best hidden relic of bygone rail travel in Nottingham exists inches beneath busy traffic across surprisingly large parts of the City.

Standard gauge horse drawn trams operated in the City in the latter half of the Nineteenth Century but in 1901, the Nottingham Corporation inaugurated its new electric tram system. In scenes that would be repeated a century later (see Chapter 5), whole streets were ripped up to accommodate laying new 112lb / foot rails, their concrete foundations, and power feeds for the new system. Depots and workshops were constructed around the City, and for the next 35 years, trams were a cheap and frequent alternative to suburban rail services.

From 1927, with major renewals of vehicles and permanent way needed, trams were gradually replaced by trolley buses. Eventually, the decision was taken to convert all remaining routes to motor buses. The last Corporation tram ran in 1936.

The overhead system was adapted to carry wires for the trolley buses, and the majority of the rails were simply left in the road. In post-war years, the growth in motorised road traffic saw the city roads surfaced with asphalt, and the rails and granite setts were buried and largely forgotten.

They would probably have stayed that way, had motor traffic not grown to the point where road layouts needed complete revision to handle unforeseen volumes of traffic, or reconstruction to cope with heavier vehicles. In the past decade, Highway Authority schemes have uncovered a number of sections of old tram rails. Analysis of what was found showed a surprisingly sophisticated design that bears many parallels with modern trackform designs for systems like the Nottingham Express Transit (NET).

Sadly the requirements of these road schemes have led to removal of these relics of the long lost transport system. There are still many places however, where the rails remain, and will probably do so for decades to come.

The Author managed a number of these schemes, and the photographs that follow are a representative sample of what was found, together with a few other reminders of Nottingham's first electric trams.

Overleaf top : This unattributed 1930s photograph shows an Arnold-bound Corporation tram on Milton Street. In the years before widespread car ownership, it was safe to walk into the middle of the road, in order to board the tram.

Overleaf Below : A set of points were uncovered at the bottom of Angel Row during construction of NET. The trench in which they were found was to accommodate a new kerb, and the rails were cut out with an oxy-acetylene torch.

Two Edwardian rail engineering legacies. Tram rails heading for Trent Bridge are seen outside A E Lambert's 1904 Midland Station on Carrington Street. The rails were uncovered during strengthening works to the bridge over the railway in 2007.

Above ground elements of the old tram system today enjoy a degree of protection under planning restrictions, and a number of building fixings for the overhead are still in place, including this one in Wheeler Gate.

A reminder of the Corporation Tramways and the origins of present day Nottingham City Transport can be found on the corner of Parliament Street bus depot. Built in 1926 to house trams and trolley buses, it currently serves a large part of the City's bus fleet.

In 2007, reminders of Nottingham's first electric trams abound at Parliament Street Depot. The rail grooves are filled with concrete, but these tracks are still clearly visible.

Tram rails on Upper Parliament Street in 2002. These were uncovered by Carillion, working on the Nottingham Express Transit (NET) project.

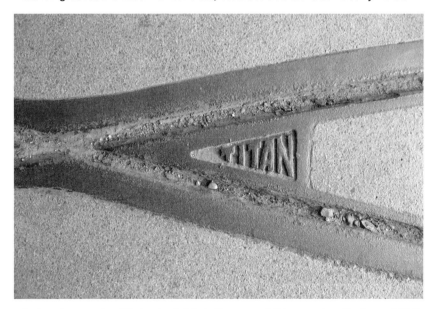

A manufacturer's name is still clearly visible in the nose of this crossing. Parliament St Depot was not opened until 1926, and so the good condition of this trackwork is perhaps a reflection of it having less than ten years use before trams were abolished in the city.

4.0 Special Selection

Special Workings in and around Nottingham

Not all passenger trains on the public railway appear in the published timetables. Special trains and excursions have been a feature of railway operation for almost as long as there have been railways, and certainly predate the preservation era. This Chapter records just a few of the special workings to have passed through the Nottingham area over the past 40 years or so.

When it was obvious that time was running out for steam and numerous lines alike in the 1960s, specials became more commonplace. Enthusiasts sought to experience the spectacle of main line steam whilst they could, and to travel routes that would soon disappear. Motive power was often exotic or unusual to the area, and some of these workings are captured in the pages that follow.

The Seventies saw little in the way of steam specials, with a complete ban on main line steam working at one point. Attitudes in officialdom gradually changed however, and in the Eighties a number of steam specials visited the City. Since then occasional special workings have graced Nottingham, and with fascination for steam traction continuing unabated, this seems set to continue indefinitely.

Unusual motive power on the Midland Railway's Lincoln Line. GWR No 4965 'Rood Ashton Hall' is seen near Burton Joyce with a railtour bound for Lincoln on 31st March 2007.

A pair of DRS Class 20s has just departed from the eastern end of Nottingham Station, and cross the Nottingham Canal with an excursion bound for Skegness on 29th August 2007.

Class 8F No 48467 passes London Road Low Level Station in the rain with an eastbound special working on 26th March 1966. The blue and grey BR Mk II coach is of interest.

Rob Hancock

72

Stanier Duchess No 46251 'City of Nottingham' is recorded here at Nottingham Victoria on 5th May 1964. The locomotive was working an RCTS Special, 'The East Midlander', and the train was bound for Eastleigh and Swindon (although the locomotive was taken off the train at Didcot). The locomotive was based at Crewe North Shed, and this was its first visit to its namesake city. One of the nameplates from this engine is preserved at Wollaton Hall Industrial Museum (see Chapter 2), Sadly the locomotive itself was withdrawn from service and cut up for scrap not long after this photograph was taken.

Rob Hancock

35030 Elder Dempster Lines heads the LCGB Great Central Railtour south past Weekday Cross Junction on the last day of the GC main line. 3/9/66.

Rob Hancock

Preserved A3 4472 'Flying Scotsman' at Nottingham Victoria with the return leg of the 'Great Central Special' special working, from Marylebone to Manchester. 15th June 1963.

Rob Hancock

This October 1965 view shows the RCTS Midland Requiem Railtour in charge of the last Class 4F No 43935, slowing to take the west to north curve at Lenton South Junction.

Rob Hancock

The return leg of the special working to Lincoln of 31/3/07 is seen here at Stoke Bardolph. This locomotive was assembled from parts of 4965 'Rood Aston Hall', and No 4983 'Albert Hall' by BR workshops in the early 1960s, and for many years assumed the latter identity.

Stanier Class 5 No 44932 stands at Burton Joyce Station with an eastbound steam special on a chilly February morning in 1989.

Seen from Lenton Lane overbridge, Castle Class No 7029 'Clun Castle' passes Lenton South Junction with an Ian Allen Railtour in March 1965.

Rob Hancock

GW (actually a 1950 BR built engine) No 7029 Clun Castle presents a fine sight at Newark, on the East Coast Main Line, with a Newcastle-bound special in October 1967.

Rob Hancock

West Country Class No 34002 'Salisbury' makes an atmospheric sight at Nottingham Victoria as it departs to the south with a Great Central railtour in August 1966.

Rob Hancock

After withdrawal from service and restoration to LNER livery, A3 Pacific 4472 Flying Scotsman worked numerous railtours, including several on the Great Central. It is seen here running into Nottingham Victoria from the north end in 1963.

Rob Hancock

Flying Scotsman is seen at Newark Northgate in 1969 with a northbound special working. The bell and whistle attached to the front of the engine were acquired for its American tour.

Newark Advertiser

Viewed here from the trackside, 4474 draws admiring glances from the crowded platform at Nottingham Victoria. This was the locomotives first visit to Nottingham after its restoration.

Rob Hancock

A final view of Flying Scotsman, through a telephoto lens, again on the ECML, this time at Hougham, to the north of Newark in 1982. Note the enthusiasts at the trackside.

Author

One final look at a special working, this time on a more sombre occasion. The 3rd September 1966 was the final day of operation for the Great Central as a main line. Local services and freight would linger for a few more years, but the days of Marylebone expresses had ended. 35030 Elder Dempster Line worked an RCTS Railtour over the route on what was to be the only occasion that a rebuilt Merchant Navy visited the city. The location is the site of Wilford Brickworks sidings. The signal box that controlled these is gutted and awaiting demolition.

Rob Hancock

5.0 Nottingham Express Transit

Line One and Beyond

One might perhaps ask whether a work on railway history is perhaps an appropriate platform from which to write about a modern tram system. Today's projects are tomorrow's history however, and developing Nottingham Express Transit (NET) has had a profound effect on the City, bringing rail based transport into its heart, and affecting the way that many thousands of people commute.

NET is one of a new generation of standard gauge light rail systems, of which there are about a half-dozen or so, nationally, at present. This chapter takes an in depth look at how the project was procured, and how it was designed and built. It looks at some of the problems that were encountered along the way, and how these were overcome. It also considers future developments, and what additions to the network can be expected in the coming years.

5.1 Origins, Funding and Development

NET was initially promoted by a partnership of Nottinghamshire County and Nottingham City Councils, together with Nottingham Development Enterprise (NDE). It was seen as the answer to growing traffic congestion in the Greater Nottingham area, and a stimulus to economic growth in areas that had suffered historically from underinvestment, and loss of jobs. From inception in the 1980s, the County were the lead organisation and, from 1988, it was they, with support from the partnership and specialist consultants that procured funding for the development of the project. They produced the initial designs for the route, obtained Parliamentary Powers, acquired land and put together a tender package for delivery of the detailed design of the system (including trams).

In 1998, local government reorganisation saw Nottingham revert to being a unitary status council, and leadership of the project (together with many of the personnel working on it) transferred from the County Council to the City Council.

In 2000 the concession for carrying forward the design, building, financing and ultimately operating the system was awarded jointly by the City and County Councils to Arrow Light Rail Ltd, a consortium of companies. This comprised the civil engineering contractor, Carillion PLC, train maker Adtranz (now Bombardier), Nottingham City Transport, the area's primary bus operator, and international transport systems operator Transdev.

The funding of the construction work was achieved through a Private Finance Initiative (PFI) and the consortium signed to a 30 year concession to operate the system, and recover its upfront £180M construction costs, together with financing and operating costs through performance linked service availability payments, passenger revenues and associated income. At the end of this period, the assets would revert to the local authorities.

Below : Plan of the street running section of NET Line One. Integration of the system into a busy city centre was a difficult challenge, overcome by careful forward planning and innovative contractual arrangements.

Plan Courtesy Nottingham City Council

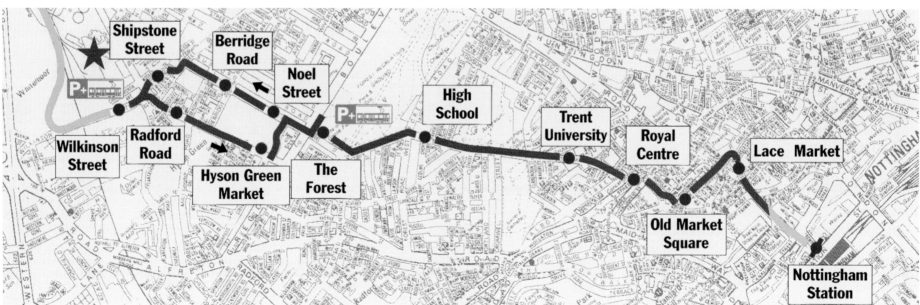

At 4.50am on Sunday 20th July 2003 history was made when No 214 became the first tram to venture onto the City's streets for 67 years. NET General Manager Andy Wood was at the controls and an army of engineers and officials were in attendance.

At its southern end, NET follows the route of the Great Central Main Line. The view above shows a southbound special crossing the viaduct in 1966. The viaduct was demolished in 2000 (below) to make way for a new structure to carry NET.

(Top photo Rob Hancock, Bottom Author)

5.1.2 Roles and Responsibilities

Delivery of the project was the responsibility of the concessionaire, with the local authorities having planning and design approvals. The detailed design for the tracks, tram stops and supporting infrastructure was the responsibility of Carillion. Many elements of the civil engineering design were contracted to the Manchester office of consultants Faber Maunsell. The design work was developed by these two parties, in close liaison with the City Council's Highway Authority. The trams, electrical and mechanical equipment, including the overhead line equipment were designed by Bombardier.

5.2 The Line Described

Nottingham's Express Transit system (NET) was a project that in some respects looked simultaneously in both directions. A mass rapid transit system for the 21st Century was designed and built to utilise not only city streets but also elements of 19th Century railway lines. Line One was designed to link Hucknall to the City Centre and incorporated elements of the old Midland, Great Northern and the Great Central Railways. The route is double track as far north as Bulwell, with the remainder consisting single track with passing loops.

— FRONT ELEVATION. —

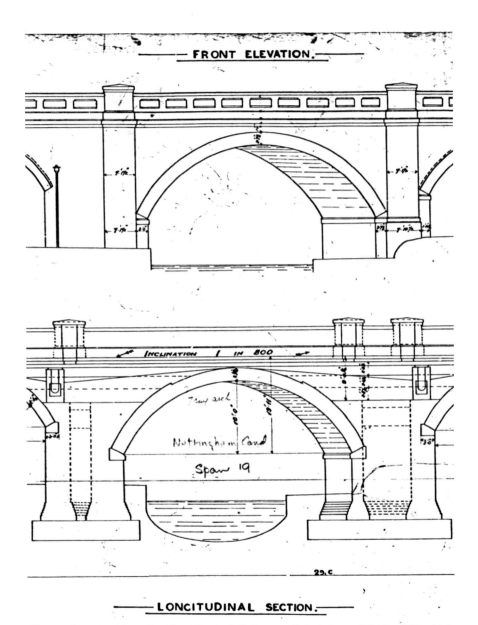

INCLINATION 1 IN 800

Nottingham Canal

Span 19

— LONGITUDINAL SECTION. —

30/10/2007 10:27

Above : An extract from the Great Central' Railways original plans of Bridge 287, which included the crossing of the Nottingham Canal.

Opposite : This short section of the old GCR structure was incorporated into NET Line One. Twenty-five years separates these views, the first of which was taken in 1982. The additional width required for platforms necessitated the construction of a reinforced concrete cantilevered deck above the original structure.

Middle Hill was built in the 1970s, and controversially cut through the line of the much lamented Drury Hill. Carried by a privately owned structure, the road over-sails parts of the Broadmarsh Shopping Centre, together with the final remains of Drury Hill. Part of this historic thoroughfare can still be viewed, together with sandstone caves from the basement of the Centre. Connecting the NET viaduct to this structure proved technically demanding, and the 1970s construction required careful assessment, and selective strengthening, to allow trams to run onto it.

From Middle Hill, north to Hyson Green, NET threads its way through the City's streets, sharing some areas with general traffic, others with pedestrians, and some zones are exclusively reserved for trams. The street plan of Nottingham is a curious jumble of elements. The City has undergone several phases of change and elements of the medieval, Victorian and 20th century layouts are laid one on top of the other, in a relatively small space. To fit into this, it was necessary to take the tram lines through some of the tightest horizontal curves in the country, including an 18m radius curve from Victoria Street into Fletcher Gate. The road layout was entirely revised along the whole of the tram route, to allow trams and road vehicles to safely interact, and several roads went over to one-way or were closed to road traffic to accommodate NET.

Vehicle No 208 undergoes clearance checks in the summer of 2003, as it runs on to the new structure at Middle Hill. The tram is standing on the transition structure that spans between the new viaduct and the hidden bridge carrying the road over the Broadmarsh Centre. NETs fleet of trams number consecutively, following on from the numbers used by the original Nottingham Corporation fleet, the last of which retired in 1936.

At its southern extremity, the first half kilometre of route follows the line and level of the Great Central's London Extension. The steel bridges that carried the GCR had disappeared long before the NET project evolved, but six spans of the old GC viaduct to the north of Station Street, including the crossing of the Beeston Canal were reused with new cantilevered parapets to carry the platforms of the terminus. Initial designs had planned to use more of the GCR structure to the north of Canal Street, but the desire for clear space beneath the structure to permit development, and the complexity of providing a connection across to Middle Hill led to the old arches being abandoned in favour of a new purpose built structure.

When first built, the NET alignment afforded a view of the GNR line from the old High Level Station, heading towards Weekday Cross Junction. The pace of development in the City is such that little trace now exists of this line, or indeed Weekday Cross Junction. Similarly the GCR tunnel entrance at Weekday Cross has also disappeared from view, hidden behind the new Contemporary Arts Centre.

Tram No 208 leaves Market Street and edges cautiously towards Beastmarket Hill on the southbound leg of a test run in 2003. These were carried out in the early hours of the morning, whilst road traffic was minimal, and before crowds of sight seers could disrupt proceedings. A police escort was in attendance, to ensure that the route was obstruction free.

After skirting around Old Market Square, the line heads up Market Street, following part of the route taken by the 1901 Corporation Tramway. Excavation work for the construction of NET found many remnants of the earlier system, including a complete set of points, buried within later road construction, by the corner of Market Street and Angel Row.

It is not just trackwork that survived from the old system. In common with NET, the overhead wires were supported from building fixings wherever possible. The NET fixings are discrete masonry anchor bolts, but the Corporation Tramways utilised relatively ornate cast anchor plates, and many remain in place and can still be seen around the City, if you know where to look.

Closure of the bottom of Wollaton Street allowed the creation of a new public square outside the Theatre Royal, with a tram stop to one side. Tram platforms were designed here, as with other locations, to blend into footways, and to cause as little disruption to adjacent properties and accesses as possible. NET runs along the side of the theatre, past the stage door. An unloading bay was built next to the rails, but vehicles unloading props and equipment need to be mindful of the trams. The rails here are constructed on a vibration absorbing polymer mat, to minimise disturbance to the Royal Centre and the Theatre by passing trams.

The tram signals on the approaches to the busy Parliament Street junction are, in common with all other sites along the route, interlinked with the traffic signals to ensure there is no conflict between road traffic and trams.

Travelling north past Nottingham Trent University, the Arboretum and Nottingham High School for Boys, the route reaches The Forest. This is the site of the world famous Goose Fair, and the only on-street tram stop to have three platforms. The system's only set of gauntleted points are also found at this location, keeping the switch blades clear of traffic on the busy Gregory Boulevard.

Heading north again, the 'up' and 'down' lines split and take different routes through Hyson Green, before rejoining at Wilkinson Street, close to the system's depot, and around the corner from Shipstone's famous Star Brewery.

From Wilkinson Street, NET leaves the roads and picks up the Midland Railway's Leen Valley route, reopened to passengers as the 'Robin Hood Line' in 1993. Running to the west of the railway lines, it follows the formation of sidings that were once opposite the Basford Gas works, and served a long defunct Council Depot, before passing beneath the Ring Road and Church Street using redundant spans of existing rail structures.

Left : When excavating for the new kerblines at the junction of Angel Row and Beastmarket Hill, a fan of points from the original tram system were uncovered. The rails were in remarkably good condition and originally formed part of the junction complex between Angel Row, Long Row, Beastmarket Hill and Market Street. The rails within the area of excavation were burned out with oxy-acetylene cutters so that the work could proceed.

Top : Clearance tests at The Forest in August 2003. The platform coping stones were not put in place until the swept path of the trams could be accurately determined. The dimension has a theoretically value, but the sideplay of the vehicle made this difficult to set out. Eventually the copings were set to gauge by parking a tram at the stop, and measuring the clearance to the vehicle. The tram nearest the camera is missing its protruding steps beneath the doors. These were only fitted once the platform coping had been fixed in place.

Above : Further north on Line One, the route passed through the site of the Midland Railway's Basford Vernon Station . This had closed in the wake of the Beeching Report in 1964. The old station footbridge remained in place carrying a public right of way, until the construction of NET. It is seen here just prior to removal in 2001. A longer structure with access ramps now spans both NET and the Robin Hood Line at this location, giving access to Basford tramstop.

A view south from the same footbridge in 1962. The present day NET stop occupies the site of the Down platform, through which a Worksop bound train is seen passing.

Tony Hill

Enabling works had already begun at Lincoln Street crossing when this view was recorded in 2001. Fresh ballast is visible on the Robin Hood line, where a crossing had been removed. In the photograph, new crossing lights ('wig-wags') are in the process of being installed, and the crossing will shortly change over to CCTV operation from Trent Power Box.

By spring 2002 works to the Robin Hood line were complete and track laying for NET was well under way. The old Midland Railway signal box had been removed. The platforms for NET's David Lane stop had yet to be constructed and some of the rail mounted equipment is visible in the background. The Class 156 unit is destined for Worksop, and about to pass a southbound Class 170 which has just left the single track section.

Passing through the site of Basford Vernon's goods yard, NET runs into the first "Off-street" stop, on the site of the old railway station. The construction of this was facilitated by demolition of the original Midland Railway brick goods shed, the wrought iron station footbridge and last traces of the station's Down platform. Parts of the Up platform and the waiting room survived the disturbance during construction work, but these have now sadly disappeared too.

North from Basford the line reaches David Lane (Lincoln Street Crossing), and rail and tram routes have interlinked but independent crossings of the highway, immediately next to a busy road junction. The arrangement is unique in the country and both tram and rail lights are connected to the road junction traffic lights. From 1916 until 2002, a Midland Railway Type 2a signal box guarded the crossing. The box was unusual in that it was narrower than the standard Midland pattern, to fit the tight location. Displaced to accommodate the new crossing arrangements, it escaped demolition being removed in two sections to Serco's signal training facility at Leicester. It is now used to train signalling technicians on mechanical box faults.

The Midland line had been double track as far as Bestwood Park Junction after it's reopening as the Robin Hood Line, but in order to facilitate the construction of NET, it was singled from just south of Bulwell Station. The end of Calverton Colliery traffic and improved signalling mitigated for the reduction in track capacity, and the formation freed up allowed NET to squeeze alongside, avoiding the need for land-take.

Before reaching Bulwell, the line passes the site of Basford Junction. Here, branch lines for Bennerley and for Cinderhill Colliery at one time diverged to the west. The Bennerley line was closed in stages from 1916, and finished entirely in the 1960s. The Cinderhill line closed in the 1980s, after closure of the colliery that it served.

By the 1990s little remained at Basford Junction, other than two truncated spurs. The Cinderhill branch was selected to form a single track branch from the main route to a new park and ride site on former colliery land, close to Junction 26 of the M1.

56041 approaches Cinderhill Colliery, passing the site of the junction with the Great Northern's spur from the Derbyshire Extension. Today this is the location of the Cinderhill tram stop, and the NET platform now stands where the ground frame is situated in this view dated 3rd May 1979. Prior to abandonment of the GNR link in 1968, a Midland Railway signal cabin stood in the apex of the junction.

Graham Jelly

At Bulwell, NET drops to single track, to negotiate Highbury Vale overbridge, sharing the single span with the Robin Hood Line. The two single track lines then follow the old Leen Valley Line formation, crossing Carey Road, at Bulwell Forest, on a shared level crossing.

At Moorbridge, the Robin Hood Line was slued to make room for NET, and the BR built Bestwood Park Jn Signal Box was demolished to make space for the tram stop. The mothballed line to Calverton Colliery remained in situ, and the last few semaphore signals on the heavy rail line were replaced with coloured lights.

At Butler's Hill, the route occupies part of the Great Northern Railway's Leen Valley Branch formation that once ran adjacent to the Midland. Here the GN built a halt, and very close to the old location, a tram stop of the same name was built.

A short distance north, the line runs into the terminus at Hucknall, with the Robin Hood Line Station alongside. The tram station occupies part of the site of the old Hucknall Byron Station, and prior to construction of NET, the approach road was still flanked by distinctive Midland Railway cast iron lamp posts, and a small section of the old stone faced island platform remained next to the pier beneath the two span overbridge.

Remodelling and construction of car parking facilities during the building of NET saw these reminders of earlier days finally disappear, but in their place Hucknall, and Nottingham gained a fast, reliable light rail route that is today the envy of many other cities.

5.3 Designing the Infrastructure

5.3.1 Track Construction

NET is laid to standard gauge (1495mm) and uses two types of running rail. Conventional BS80A flat bottomed rail is used in "off-street" areas, in combination with concrete sleepers and ballasted track. SEI 40A grooved rail with ALH Polymer coating is used "on-street", set into a concrete track slab. The polymer coating provides a resilient interface between the concrete and rail, and helps reduce stray current leakage into the surrounding construction.

Rails were welded together using the 'Thermit' process, and, after grinding and ultrasonic tests, the joints were insulated with site mixed polymer compound, poured into an in-situ mould.

Design and construction of the track slabs was a significant element of the project. There are four principal types of slab construction in the street running areas, two being surfaced with bituminous material and two in concrete. Construction in trafficked areas is finished in flexible material, to blend with the road surface, whilst a concrete finish used in areas with traffic restrictions.

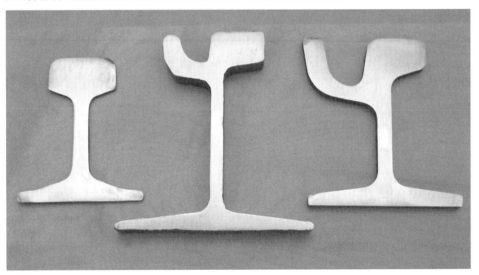

Comparative samples of tram rail. The tallest rail is 112 lb/yd section manufactured Circa 1901 for the Nottingham Corporation Tramway by a Sheffield rolling mill. The remaining samples are SEI-40A grooved rail (right) and BS80A flat bottomed rail (left) from the street running and off-street sections respectively of the Nottingham Express Transit (NET) system.

A sample panel of track was constructed in the Forest Park & Ride car park, prior to building NET, to try out proposed construction techniques and verify the buildability of the design. The concrete slab that supports the load of the tram is clearly visible in this view. The concrete used in trafficked carriageways was pigmented black on the final build, to help the tracks blend with the road surface.

i) Flexible Composite Trackform

Most of the track construction in the public highway is flexible-rigid composite. The tracks are supported by a heavily reinforced concrete (rigid) slab, made up in two layers totalling around 300mm thick. This extends to within 100mm of the surface. The remainder of the construction is bituminous (flexible) road surfacing material. The polymer coated rail is fully encased in concrete, which extends to the surface over a 100mm width to each side, forming a "shoulder", against which the bituminous surfacing is compacted and sealed. The top layer of concrete is self-coloured black in trafficked areas, and red in tram-only areas to match the colour of the surfacing.

The buried outer edge of the slab extends some 200mm beyond the visible edge of the shoulder, and the joint between lower road construction layers and the slab itself is spanned by a geotextile reinforcement layer, to stop cracking.

A hot applied joint seal prevents moisture ingress between the shoulder and the flexible surface, and was poured into a specially cut slot.

ii) Flexible Floating Trackform

This track type is used where the rails are unavoidably close to properties, or pass through sensitive environments. The basic design is similar to that described above, but the concrete slab sits on a neoprene sponge mat to absorb vibration. This mat extends up the side of the concrete slab, finishing 100mm below the surface. Mass concrete sidewalls limit lateral movement of the track slab. The flexible surfacing extends across the top, but to prevent it cracking, a surface joint is formed in poured polymer compound. These sections of trackform are readily identified by the additional narrow black strips that run parallel to the shoulder.

iii) Fully Rigid Trackform

The trackform is identifiable by its full width exposed aggregate concrete surface finish. The design is a hybrid, combining the characteristics of a continuously reinforced concrete road pavement with a reinforced concrete trackslab.

There are no movement joints in the construction, with thermal stresses being counter-acted by ground anchors. There is a centreline warping joint. This has been sawn and sealed with a Polysulphide joint sealant coloured brown. The space between the granite kerb faces and the slab edges are also sealed, to keep surface water out of the construction.

The concrete forming the upper surface is pigmented with a plum coloured dye. The surface was seeded with red granite chippings whilst still wet and these were exposed by pressure washing after the concrete had achieved an initial "set". Application of spay applied retardant after the concrete was floated permitted removal of the upper layer of matrix, leaving the chips in situ.

iv) Fully Rigid Floating Trackform

This exists at only one location on the route, alongside the Royal Centre. The detail of the vibration absorbing membrane is the same as with the flexible surfaced equivalent.

The only significant variation is the covering of the polymer joint with a natural colour calcined bauxite thermoplastic anti-skid material. The polymer was finished slightly low, and the anti-skid treatment applied as a cosmetic measure, to disguise the otherwise black jointing material.

Opposite: The four types of trackslab design used on NET Line One are shown here.

Top Left : The flexible-composite construction used where the line runs along public roads.

Top Right The "fully rigid" construction used in pedestrian priority parts of the City Centre and adjacent to the Forest tram stop by the Goose Fair site.

Bottom Left : In areas where the alignment is unavoidably close to buildings, the tracks are suspended on a raft of foam rubber matting to absorb vibration

Bottom Right : The equivalent detail as used in areas of fully rigid (concrete) construction.

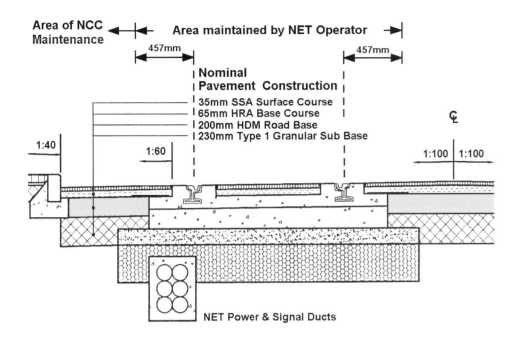

Area of NCC Maintenance

Area maintained by NET Operator

457mm

457mm

Nominal
Pavement Construction

35mm SSA Surface Course
65mm HRA Base Course
200mm HDM Road Base
230mm Type 1 Granular Sub Base

1:40

1:60

1:100 | 1:100

NET Power & Signal Ducts

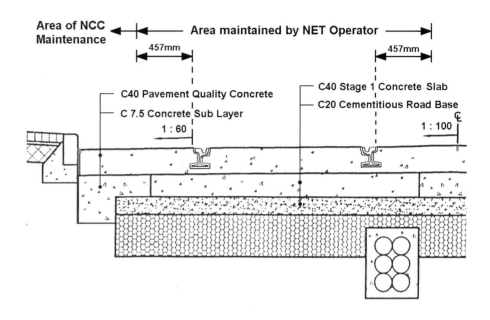

Area of NCC Maintenance

Area maintained by NET Operator

457mm

457mm

C40 Pavement Quality Concrete

C40 Stage 1 Concrete Slab

C 7.5 Concrete Sub Layer

C20 Cementitious Road Base

1 : 60

1 : 100

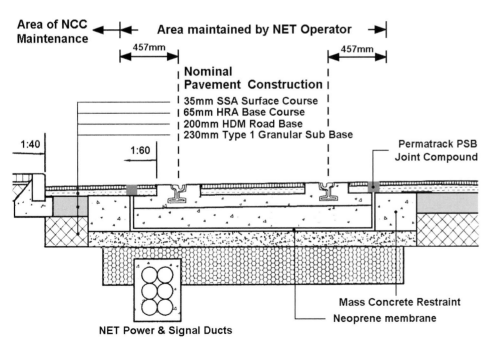

Area of NCC Maintenance

Area maintained by NET Operator

457mm

457mm

Nominal
Pavement Construction

35mm SSA Surface Course
65mm HRA Base Course
200mm HDM Road Base
230mm Type 1 Granular Sub Base

Permatrack PSB
Joint Compound

1:40

1:60

Mass Concrete Restraint

Neoprene membrane

NET Power & Signal Ducts

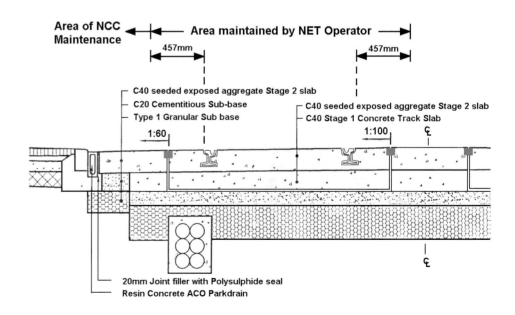

Area of NCC Maintenance

Area maintained by NET Operator

457mm

457mm

C40 seeded exposed aggregate Stage 2 slab

C20 Cementitious Sub-base

Type 1 Granular Sub base

C40 seeded exposed aggregate Stage 2 slab

C40 Stage 1 Concrete Track Slab

1:60

1:100

20mm Joint filler with Polysulphide seal

Resin Concrete ACO Parkdrain

Left : A section of Stage 1 support slab is cast on Waverley Street. The substantial reinforcement was designed to cope with the effects of variable ground conditions, and to span over any short voids that might open up beneath the slab during its lifetime. Maintaining access to properties during this phase of work was extremely difficult, as was delivering the concrete to where it was needed. This particular pour utilised a boom mounted concrete pump, the discharge pipe of which can be seen on the right of the picture. The demands of the project programme led to construction work taking place sometimes in less than ideal conditions. This particular concreting operation was interrupted by a heavy shower; drops of rain caused the blurred marks on the image.

Below Left : The junction of Radford Road and Wilkinson Street. The Stage 1 slab has cured, and the concrete has been drilled, and threaded studs fixed in place with epoxy resin. Baseplates have been attached to the studs, and the grooved rails put in place and welded up. The final geometry of the trackwork is set up at this point in the work, lifting, lowering or drifting the baseplates to achieve the required line. The next operation will be casting of the second concrete slab, which will embed the rails in place. A debonding layer is painted onto the concrete immediately below the rail, in case it is necessary to replace it at some stage in the future.

Below : After placement of the upper layer of concrete, 100mm of blacktop is laid on the top, to complete the carriageway surface. This has to be laid in narrow strips because of the gauge of the rails. The machine employed to do this was imported specially from Germany. Conventional paving machines cannot lay such narrow strips, and the Highway Authority's insistence that the surface be machine laid, to achieve optimum consolidation and a smooth finish, led to this equipment being sourced for the work. The location is Waverley Street, close to the junction with Forest Road.

Rail sections are seen here being welded together on Noel Street, using a 'Thermit' pot. Heat generated by a chemical reaction melts the steel. The section being welded has no polymer coating on it. This is cast around the rail using a special mould, after the weld has cooled, been ground and inspected.

Tram Rails and Roads

One of the greatest problems facing modern track designers is how to combine the requirements of a road with those of a railway. Key problem areas are geometry, drainage and the interaction of road vehicles with rails.

Cant or No Cant?

In the railway industry today, straight track is constructed without cant (elevation of one rail above the other. If one rail is higher than the other, a greater force is exerted on the low rail, causing it to wear more quickly. Cant is only applied to curves on higher speed lines, where it counteracts the effects of centripetal forces on the trains.

In highway construction, straight roads are generally built with a central crown, and a crossfall of 1 in 40. This enables water to flow to the edge of the road, where it can be collected in gullies. The suspension components of road vehicles are also set up to provide optimum performance at this angle. During the design development of NET, there was heated debate on how to tackle the problem of conflicting requirements. The solution lay in a compromise, with 1 in 100 adopted as a standard crossfall between rails, and the road element beyond the outside tram rail steepening to 1 in 60.

Geometry

Railways and to a lesser degree tramways are intolerant of abrupt changes in line or level. Roads on the other hand are very flexible in this respect. The line or level of an established road may be influenced by many factors, including the positions of existing buildings, local natural changes in ground level, large trees, underground obstructions and joining side roads.

In mapping the tram's vertical alignment onto the existing road network, it was found that considerable work was needed to make it fit, such that practically every road that the tram passed along needed to be completely reconstructed, together with many side road junctions. In a number of cases, retaining walls were needed to raise or lower the road to fit the alignment of the rails. The works entailed a large number of road closures, diversions and considerable disruption. Operations were carefully planned to allow premises to be accessed during the work, and businesses to continue to operate.

The final precise level of the road surface was dictated by small scale adjustments to the rails once in situ, by means of bolted down rail fixings.

A base plate for the flat bottomed rail section is seen here. The rail itself has a thick polymer coating to it. The stud to the rear bolts the assembly to the concrete support slab, and it is adjusted to height by steel shims placed underneath.

Drainage

When rain falls on a railway, it percolates through the ballast to the sand blanket of the sub-formation. This has a crossfall, and the water is shed to the sides, where it ultimately collects in a ditch or filter drain. A similar arrangement to this drains the NET formation north of Wilkinson Street, but the street-running sections faced a unique problem.

On a road, water runs across the surface to the channel at the side. It is bounded by the kerb and flows to a gully. If grooved tram rails are introduced to the surface, as much as 80% of the water is intercepted by the grooves and follows these, without actually reaching the drainage channel or gully. This will then flow to the lowest point, and can cause road and tramway to flood in storm conditions.

A variety of systems had been tried on other networks around the country, with in many cases, patchy results. When NET was being designed, the drainage method adopted on Sheffield's tram system was looked at. This comprised of a number of holes drilled though the base of the rail groove, to allow water to drain away. This arrangement however was perceived by NET's designers to be prone to blockage and a different answer had to be found.

The solution eventually chosen for NET was a combination of ideas from the design consultants and the Highway Authority. A section of the side wall of the groove in the tram rail was milled out, and a specially made access chamber attached to the side of the rail. A pipe then crossed through the trackslab and discharged into a road gully. This provided a massive increase in capacity over the Sheffield detail, and maintenance access, in the event of the drain holes become blocked. Rail drains were installed at approximately 50 metre centres.

Rail slot drains in the gauntleted track on Gregory Boulevard. This photograph was taken in heavy rain, and shows how effectively the collected water from the rails can be discharged. The access panels to the side allow for the clearance of blockages.

In service, the drainage arrangements have only been partially successful, with sand and leaves blocking the drainage slots more often than anticipated. No doubt this area will be revisited when future lines are built.

A graphic illustration of what can happen when a drainage outlet becomes blocked is seen here at Hyson Green. The grooved tram rail acts as a conduit and rapidly transfers water to the low point on the track geometry. Without an outlet, water quickly floods the tramway.

Road Traffic Interaction

An advantage to not being first in the field, is that one can learn from the experiences of others. The first tram systems to be constructed opted for positioning rails dead centre along traffic lanes. Modern cars have a track width broadly similar to standard gauge, meaning it is possible for all four wheels to be in substantial contact with smooth, friction-free tram rails, instead of the road surface. This can seriously compromise braking performance.

The solution to this was to offset the rails to one side of the lane, where width allowed, so that road vehicles would not habitually run on the rails.

Another problem encountered on other systems was how flush the rails needed to be relative to the road surface. In civil engineering, there is no such thing as zero tolerance when dealing with materials such as concrete and asphalt.

The tram rails on Waverley Street are offset relative to the traffic lane, discouraging cars from driving with their tyres on the slippery rails.

Unfortunately the Tramways Act of 1870 states that rails should be level with the road surface, and this particular piece of obscure legislation was resurrected during a hearing that followed an accident where a vehicle lost control on a tram rail on the Sheffield system that stood proud of the general surface.

Consequently huge care was taken during final construction stages that the rail head was kept as flush as reasonably possible, and many thousands of measurements were made to ensure that NET would not fall foul of the same legislation.

Not just cars have problems with tram rails. Cyclists can have tremendous difficulty with grooved rails. If a front wheel enters a groove, it snatches, the cyclist cannot adjust his balance, and invariably falls off. This can be especially serious if it occurs in traffic. The problem was anticipated at the design stage, and segregated cycle routes that kept clear of the tram rails were included. Where cycles needed to cross the lines, the crossing points were made as oblique as possible (ideally perpendicular), to minimise risk.

One further consideration related to the appearance of tram rails in an asphalt road surface. The tram lines generally follow the line of the road, but there are areas where the tram alignment diverges from that of the road. If the tram rails were visually prominent, there could be a danger of motorists following the rails rather than the road. The design incorporates a 100mm wide concrete shoulder to each side, and in order to reduce its conspicuity, the concrete mix was pigmented black, and the surface was pressure washed to expose the aggregate. The aggregate included crushed granite, to enhance the surface texture, and to assist in giving a final appearance that was as close to road surfacing as possible.

5.3.2 The Overhead Line Equipment

The overhead electrification on NET operates at 750V DC, with a single overhead conductor, and return via the rails.

In the street running section, OLE comprises a single copper conductor, generally supported by a headspan wire or single register. On the off-street sections, the conductor is supported by drop wires from a catenary support wire, similar to the arrangement used in heavy rail practice. In common with heavy rail systems, the wire zig-zags in plan slightly to even out wear on the carbon strips on the pantograph heads.

Erection of a register to carry the overhead contact wire is seen here at Shipstone Street, in Hyson Green. The tubular steel pole supporting the overhead is bolted to a piled foundation.

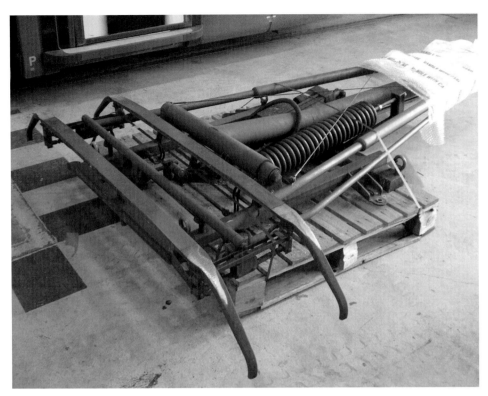

A pantograph is seen at close quarters in NET's Wilkinson Street Depot. The units are periodically removed for maintenance and renewal of the contact surface on the head. One spare serviceable unit is kept available at the depot at all times.

Whilst the OLE is supported by building fixings in the City Centre, this was not possible for the majority of the route, and mini-piles were augered, and capped with in-situ concrete encasing anchor cradles. These required careful placement to avoid buried utility apparatus, foundations and projecting cellars.

The technique proved successful, with only a couple of failures (out of several hundred) on poles that were subject to particularly high lateral forces. These occurred during construction and were associated with unexpected local variation in ground conditions (in once case a buried cellar from a long demolished property) and no problems have arisen in service.

One unusual aspect of having live overhead on the public highway is the requirement for maintenance to street lights. This operation would usually be carried out from an access platform, but the presence of live wires makes it impossible. Consequently all lighting columns on the route were designed to be hinged near the base, and to fold in a direction that didn't conflict with overhead poles or other street furniture.

Stray Currents

The effects of induced current were not entirely understood by the builders of the early electric tramways. In essence, any electric current generates a magnetic field. Similarly, any conductor inside this magnetic field will have a secondary flow of electrons generated within it. This conductor could be a steel duct, copper cable, or indeed anything metallic. Electrons in the secondary conductor find their way to earth, and electrolytic corrosion of the conductor takes place. Current leakage on early electric tramways caused corrosion of anything in close proximity and metallic conductors for the GPO's telephone circuits in particular suffered severe problems. These were the subject of a legal battle with the Glasgow Corporation tramways in the 1940s that ultimately led to that system closing.

The modern generation of light rail systems benefit from a better understanding of the problem. Measures taken to avoid it include electrical bonding of the steel reinforcement in the concrete slab that supports the rails, and return of any collected current to the system. Tram rails are insulated with a thick polymer layer to reduce leakage, and any major iron covers required in the immediate track area are similarly insulated. Any utilities that run in the highway are generally diverted well away from the tracks prior to construction, to avoid induced currents.

5.3.3 The Trams

NET operates a fleet of 15 trams. These fully low floored vehicles were manufactured by Bombardier at Derby, to their Incentro design, and when built were amongst the most advanced units in the world. They have seating accommodation for 62 passengers, standing space for a similar number, and two designated wheelchair spaces.

Much of the electrical equipment is mounted on the roof, and there are no continuous axles on the wheel sets, freeing up floor space inside. The outer bogies are driven, and the traction control is digitally linked to automatic sanding gear and to the braking system.

Like some of their heavy rail cousins, the trams operate a regenerative braking system, and current generated is returned to the system. This is augmented by hydraulic and electromagnetic braking systems. Each tram has 8 motors, one for each wheel of the outer bogies. Each 33m long unit comprises 5 segments, and has three "bogies", leaving two sections "floating" in space.

The internal layout design was derived from detailed public consultation exercises, and a full scale mock-up was constructed and displayed in the Old Market Square before the real units were built. Special attention was given to provision for the mobility impaired, and people with pushchairs, as well as the needs of the visually impaired.

The interior of a brand new tram in early 2003, just after delivery from Bombardier's Derby works. Experience in service has led to a number of minor modifications to be made, including installation of CCTV cameras on board.

A partly stripped traction bogie is seen in the NET workshop at Wilkinson Street. Each wheel is mounted on an individual stub axle, allowing the low floor arrangement in the tram.

The driver's "rear view mirrors" are television cameras mounted high up on each cab, and small screens on the panel give a view of the vehicle's exterior. An electronic "bell" warns pedestrians of the tram approaching or pulling away, and an air horn is available. Although the trams can only travel in a fixed path, indicators are fitted, so that a stationary tram can signal to traffic that it is about to start moving. Route selection is possible at points, and the driver controls the operation of these, with buttons on the console to select the route to be taken.

The wheel design for the trams incorporates two-step coning, and has a flange profile suited to flange running on switches and crossings, although flange running does not take place on the system. During early trials, a couple of minor derailments sparked internal debate about rail/wheel compatibility, but modification of several sets of points solved the problem, and a couple of years down the line, the operation of NET has been incident free.

The public consultation exercise also revealed a preference for old style conductors on the new trams, and this preference suited Arrow's concerns about potential fare evasion. Consequently, when they entered service in 2004, each vehicle carried at least one conductor. In busy times, it has been found useful for further conductors to sell tickets at the tram stops.

The Tram Stops

The low floor design of the trams allowed the platforms to be less obtrusive than examples on other systems, however it was still necessary to build platforms with 370mm high faces, compared with a normal kerb height of 125mm.

In street running areas, the platforms are part of the footway, and tram stop equipment such as shelters, lighting, real time tram information displays and litter bins are neatly integrated with conventional street furniture. Public address systems allow announcements to be made, in the event of unscheduled delays.

Old Market Square tram stop awaits its first revenue earning service. Sunday 7th March 2004.

Those platforms in the immediate City Centre were completed with York Stone paving to match the surrounding area, whilst concrete flag paving was used elsewhere. In common with many other aspects of NET, every detail was carefully developed, and then scrutinised by the Railway Inspectorate (HMRI). Consultation with disability user groups led to inclusion of special tactile paving surfaces to enable the visually impaired to locate the help-point system, and wheelchair logos were designed into the platform surface at the locations where the double width doors would be, with the tram at rest in the platform.

5.4 Construction

The logistics of any construction project the size of NET are daunting, and the following selection of considerations is just a representative sample of what went into the project.

Diversion of Utilities

Prior to any construction work taking place, it is necessary to relocate water mains, telephone lines, electricity cables and gas mains. In the case of NET this took several years to plan and coordinate between the various companies, and 18 months to accomplish. Temporary traffic signals, footway and lane closures, and traffic diversions were to give local residents and businesses a taste of the main works to come.

Avoiding Hidden Pitfalls

If a project hasn't been properly researched, all manner of problems can turn up during construction work. On the NET project, considerable effort went into reviewing Local Authority records, old maps and ground investigation data, at the design stage. This "Desktop Study" revealed all sorts of interesting pitfalls, including Victorian service tunnels running under parts of the route, basements and cellars of long demolished buildings, caves in the sandstone below and, ironically, the remains of tracks from Nottingham's first electric tram system that had been abandoned before the Second World War.

Old tram rails make way for new outside the Theatre Royal on Upper Parliament Street in 2002.

Any one of these issues could have delayed progress, but a robust design process was able to take them into account. Mitigation in the design included making the concrete slab that supported the rails strong enough to span over voids below. In the case of the brick tunnels in Market Street and Victoria Street, the tunnels were assessed, and additional reinforcement was incorporated to allow for fitting a thinner slab above the crowns of the arches.

A minor problem that almost slipped through the net related to a small area of wetland traversed by the route. It is a requirement of the Wildlife & Countryside Act that such sites are checked for protected species such as the Great Crested Newt. Although identified early in the project, this area was inadvertently omitted from the construction plans and when work started, it was unclear whether the pond had been checked for protected species. A specialist was hurriedly called in, and was able to confirm that none were present. The design was quickly revised to allow for the local ground conditions, and the work pushed on.

Rail Deliveries

Unlike conventional rails, tram rails have a specific orientation owing to their grooved profile. When delivered to site in an urban environment, they are generally too long to turn around in the street, should they arrive facing the wrong way around. Similarly, rails formed to specific radii had to be correctly identified before placement, to ensure the correct geometry was attained, much like putting together a giant train set. Fortunately careful planning by Carillion's engineers meant that there were few embarrassments.

Bridging the Gap

With the best will in the world sometimes mistakes are made, causing difficulties on site. An example that caused a few red faces was the erection of the footbridge connecting Station Street tram stop to the Nottingham Railway Station. The design had been prepared and checked. The bridge had been fabricated off site, and then brought in for erection. The road was closed to allow a crane to lift it into place.

Everything went like clockwork, until the bridge was lowered into position, and found not to fit the gap properly. The steelwork had been constructed with small variances in the skew angle and span length, which were enough to result in the ends of the beams missing their bearings, to leave a significant gap between the abutment and the deck.

The structure was temporarily propped whilst a solution was sought. Eventually specially fabricated fillets were welded to the beam ends, allowing them to rest safely on the bearings. The decking was similarly extended to close the gap, allowing the footbridge to be completed.

The troublesome north bearing of the completed footbridge over Station Street. This will form the starting point for the eventual extension of the route south.

Plugging the Hole

Another mishap involved a void that was found whilst excavating for the track slab on Goldsmith Street. This was filled with several wagon loads of concrete, the tracks built over it, and the road reinstated. A short while later it became apparent that foul drains to nearby properties were backing up. An investigation found that the void was actually a broken main sewer, and this was now filled with concrete.

There was nothing for it but to close the road again, dig up everything, excavate and relay 30m of sewer, then build a fresh section of track slab.

An Unplanned Water Feature

It wasn't just the primary engineering works that ran into snags. The scheme included dozens of trees to be planted in the City Centre. One notable mishap at the top of Pelham Street was the breeching of a water main, when anchoring the root ball of a new tree in place. This caused the loss of many thousands of gallons of water, temporarily turning Goose Gate and Hockley into a river and causing traffic chaos on Lower Parliament Street.

Some Social Problems

Unfortunately, there are some issues faced by modern construction workers that their Victorian and Edwardian counterparts didn't have to contend with.

It is common practice to securely fence work areas, to keep children from playing on the site. On Line One, vandalism of fencing proved to be a real problem in

several areas, and significant costs were incurred through damaged barriers. Construction workers were on a few occasions subjected to barrages of bottles and other missiles, whilst discarded hypodermic needles were found in several work areas. On another occasion, a setting out instrument costing thousands of pounds, complete with tripod was grabbed; the agile thief sprinting away with it tucked under his arm. The engineer had heavy site boots and a thick site coat on, and the thief had a 50 yard head start, so unsurprisingly, a clean getaway was made.

When tracks were built through the Hyson Green area, programme pressures meant that construction teams often worked into the night when laying the concrete trackform. One memorable morning, they returned to find multiple footprints down the whole length of the neatly floated slab, which had by now gone off. This incident was to be repeated on several subsequent occasions, adding to the contractor's considerable list of headaches.

Like petrified tracks in a prehistoric lake bed, footprints stretch across a cured section of concrete base slab. This problem was to repeatedly occur during the construction work.

These problems were thankfully confined to a few specific areas, and not a reflection on the diligence of the contractor, but a comment on the problems of building a piece of infrastructure in an inner-city area desperately needing investment and regeneration.

Indeed revisiting some of these areas today shows how effective the tram has been as a tool of economic regeneration. New roads, footways, lighting and street furniture are just part of the picture. Trees planted as part of the works soften the hard urban edge, and diversion of traffic away from much of the tram's route corridor has led to a quieter, safer environment, with the added benefit of a state of the art, reliable fast transport system.

Other Difficulties

Other sections of route faced different problems. Nottingham's city centre is a bustling, successful business and retail district. Shops rely on countless deliveries early each morning, and during the day, a constant stream of pedestrians crowd the city streets. Access had to be maintained to businesses for as long as possible, and work around their doorways done at night or on Sundays. Signs were put on barriers to advise customers that the businesses were open as usual, and as the works progressed, safe temporary pedestrian routes had to be made and re-made. Ramps were put in at level changes for wheelchairs and prams, warning signs erected to alert to the presence of passing vehicles, and plastic guide rails were provided for the visually impaired.

The effort on site was matched by a PR campaign led by the City's specially created Communications Team. Businesses, the travelling public, residents and just about everyone in Greater Nottingham were courted in the "charm offensive". A blizzard of leaflets and letters distributed by an army of helpers kept people in the picture about what was happening, and how long the disruption would last.

The image of this professional operation was only slightly dented when an elderly and somewhat dishevelled local "gentleman of leisure" adopted the project. What he lacked in his presentation and hygiene, he made up for in his enthusiasm. He would spend his days alternating between handing NET publicity leaflets to passers-by, that he had somehow acquired, and following around the construction crews. *("Smelly Eric" as he was referred to by the construction teams, was to prove useful on more than one occasion. He always knew more about what was happening on site than the Section Engineers, and strangely seemed to be aware of design changes and management decisions before they were even made).*

NET Line One was effectively two different construction projects. The northern section was to all intents and purposes a railway project, sharing a route corridor with the Robin Hood Line. The south half, however, was primarily a highway scheme. Railway and Highway Authorities have differing safety requirements, and problems arose due to contradictory protocols when rail contractors undertook operations on the public highway. Similarly highways personnel came into conflict with rail based staff over works on the north section, and particularly work at level crossings.

Typical differences in culture include the colour of high visibility clothing that is permitted, the ways that personnel are booked on to and off immediate work areas, and the approach taken to managing live road traffic. Even amber beacons on construction plant were a source of contention, these being mandatory on highway works, but banned on railway sites. In any large project with multiple stakeholders, objectives differ slightly and there are always teething troubles. Whilst NET had its share of these in the initial phases, as the project progressed the designers, contractors and the Highway Authority came to work as a single

team, allowing minor technical problems that would have delayed other projects to be dealt with swiftly and efficiently.

5.5 Commissioning

Gauge runs commenced on 20th July 2003, when Tram 214 made history as being the first of the new trams to run through Nottingham's City Centre. Some limited runs had been made previously on the track paralleling the Robin Hood Line, but this was the first time a vehicle ventured onto the public highway. The first trip was made at walking pace, and started at 4.50am. It was accompanied by a police escort and a select group of engineers and officials, checking clearances to the body and underside of the vehicle. The trial was a success, and in the following weeks, further test runs were made to check operational systems.

A group of trainee drivers are seen here 'learning the road' during the commissioning phase of the project.

Looking over the drivers shoulder on a test run aboard Tram 208, in 2003. The alignment here follows the line of the old GCR route, and the dark area in the distance was the old tunnel mouth at Weekday Cross, albeit hidden from view by trees. Today this location is dominated by the City's centre for contemporary arts, built across the site of the old railway.

With this done, the first "official" run was staged for publicity purposes in September 2003. The event was organised by the City Council, with television cameras and local press waiting in Old Market Square to board this "first" run. Unfortunately due to a mix up, non-project staff had not been cleared to board a vehicle that was still technically on test. This had not been made known to the party waiting, and the tram ran through the Square without stopping. The few engineers on board waved as it disappeared into the distance and a group of red faced officials were left standing on the platform in front of the cameras.

The final five months of construction coincided with full driver training, and general commissioning of the system. The remaining construction teams now faced the additional hazard of near silent trams gliding through the middle of their construction site. An advantage of having working trams however was that supervisory project staff could use them as taxis to get between worksites, saving a great deal of walking. *(To the envy of several enthusiast friends, the author became one of the first to ride every tram in the fleet during this phase of works).*

At this stage, many of the trams lacked passenger seats, coverings protected floor finishes from dirty site boots, and filled sandbags simulated carrying a load of passengers. A shadow timetable allowed the drivers and NET's Control Centre to conduct full dress rehearsals and progressively, full interiors were fitted to the vehicles, ready for opening to the public, on Tuesday 9th March, 2004.

Opening Day

NET was formally opened by the Secretary of State for Transport, Alistair Darling, on the 8th March 2004. The preceding weekend had been a frantic last minute clear up by the contractor, with the last of the major outstanding work having been completed the week before. Despite heavy rain over the weekend, everything was tidied up and ready for the big event by the Sunday evening.

The Author's immediate colleagues from the construction supervision team at the Highway Authority await the arrival of a northbound tram on opening day, Left to right, Richard Childs, John Parry, Shamala Evans, Simon Carter and Jim Codrington.

The Secretary of State met civic officials mid-morning on the 8th March, and a brief ceremony was conducted in the Old Market Square in front of local press, before the obligatory round of speeches were made by local dignitaries and politicians to guests in the City's Exchange Building. Champagne and canapés followed, and through the remainder of the day, trams gave rides to invited guests and project staff between Old Market Square and Bulwell.

After a celebratory reception for the project staff at the Hard Rock Café in Nottingham that evening, all and sundry retired to contemplate what the first day of real operation would bring.

The then Secretary of State for Transport Alistair Darling can be readily identified with his distinctive white hair, as he faces the cameras and formally opens NET on 8th March 2004.

Those who spent more than a decade developing and promoting the project, and making it a reality might measure the project as having achieved all of its major objectives, and point to the awards that the system has won since its inauguration.

The operational reality is that NET stands virtually alone in the field, as a commercial success. From the outset, trams were crowded, and despite some gloomy predictions from many within the industry, operating revenues have turned a surplus from Day 1. Indeed riding the tram today during peak hours is a not dissimilar experience to riding London's tube, a demonstration of how intensively it is used.

The success of NET is a combination of factors including careful route planning and a well thought out design, but perhaps the key element has been the inclusion of the local bus operator as a partner, rather than a rival. Bus routes were restructured to complement NET, and Park & Ride services connect with several major car parks along the route, allowing passengers to switch mode of transport. This theme is repeated along the Robin Hood Line, where heavy rail passengers can switch to NET at Hucknall and Bulwell, to access intermediate tram stops and the city centre. Through ticketing arrangements add to passenger convenience.

The first public service tram departed from Phoenix Park at a little before 6am, on the cold dark morning of March 9th, with a band of enthusiastic passengers on board, many who had queued for hours to be on this "first tram". TV and press accompanied this trip, and it was headline news on local television. *(The author had contemplated riding this tram, but having a woolly head from the previous day, decided a that a couple of extra hours in bed was a better idea).*

For the remainder of the week, trams continued to be packed with sightseers, and the platforms of City stops were crowded. It was to be at least a month, before any assessment could be made of whether it had met its objective in attracting commuter traffic. It had been expected that once the sight seers had lost interest, patronage might shrink. This didn't happen, however, and the trams continued to be busy.

Through ticketing past and present: Day Rider tickets for NET and NCT allow travel on either mode of transport. The LMSR sold tickets for trams in the pre-war years for excursion services that included destinations where rail links had been axed, due to competition from the Nottingham Corporation's tram system.

Secrets of Success

The relative success of NET depends on ones perspective. Those that designed and built the project might argue that the balance of risk was too heavily weighted against them, resulting in unforeseen costs that would take longer to recoup.

Other factors relate to public perception. Consultation and proactive publicity helped get the tram off to a positive start, and it seems to have gone from strength to strength, with much of the travelling public taking it to their heart. The quality of the vehicles and the segregation from general traffic in many areas has made the system less prone to delays than buses, and earned it a reputation for reliability that is hard to match. In some respects, NET has even become a tourist attraction, with many passenger journeys being accredited to people wanting to go for a ride on the tram, rather than journeying to a specific destination.

5.6 Future Destinations

NET was planned from the outset to be a system, rather than a single line. Line One has been a success, but it is not a network. How far it eventually grows remains to be seen, but in the short term, extensions to Clifton and Chilwell are expected to be completed some time after 2013. These connect to the south end of Line One, and after spanning the tracks of Midland Station, they split to run their separate routes at Arkwright Street, on the site of the old GCR station.

The Clifton Line's route takes it through the Meadows, and over the Wilford Toll Bridge, before skirting around Wilford Village, to pick up the alignment of the GC London Extension. Following the GCR, the route passes beneath the Ring Road on the reused railway bridge, before turning towards Silverdale, and cutting across farmland. Heading into Clifton, It follows Southchurch Drive through Clifton, terminating at a projected Park and Ride site close to the A453.

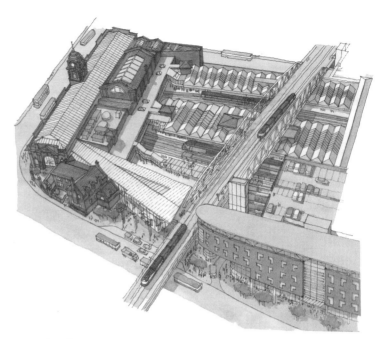

In order to extend NET south, a bridge will be required to span across the top of Nottingham Station. This will ironically sit at the same location as the GCR bowstring girder bridge that was demolished in 1980. The new structure will also be a bowstring like its predecessor, and it is hoped that the original foundations can be reused, cutting down cost and disruption.

Nottingham City Council / BDP

The route followed by the Chilwell Line heads west from Arkwright Street and through the NG2 Business Park. Rising to cross the old Midland Railway at Lenton South Junction on a new bridge, the route rejoins the public highway at Lenton Lane, before heading west to the Queens Medical Centre. It then crosses the A52 Nottingham Ring Road and skirts through the Nottingham University Campus, before running alongside University Boulevard towards Beeston, The route then heads through Chilwell to the Toton Lane Park & Ride site on the A52.

The extra services on these two new lines will require a considerable addition to the present fleet of 15 trams. It is anticipated that a further 28 would be needed, although with capacity for 50 units at the Wilkinson Street Depot, this could be achieved without provision of additional infrastructure.

As well as Phase 2, there are aspirations to extend the line east towards the Racecourse, and possibly Gedling, whilst in the west, the Phoenix Park spur may be extended towards Eastwood. The process of extending the system will not be quick, and the first of the new routes will not be completed before 2013. It is almost certain that NET will extend to Clifton and Chilwell, but even if the network remains its present size, it will still be a world class light rail system with a reputation to be envied.

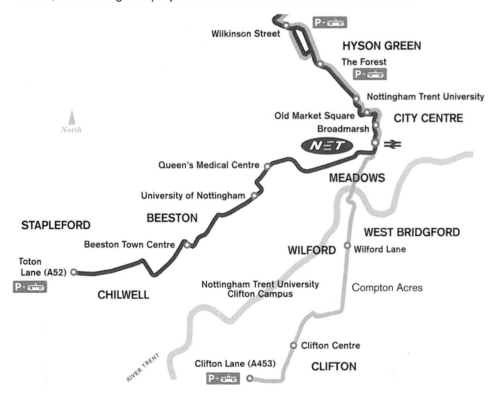

Schematic diagram of NET Phase 2 showing the proposed lines to Chilwell and Clifton.

Testing Times for NET Line One

The following photographs recorded one of the early test runs, made in August 2003. Tram 208 was selected for this particular test, and driven by Helen Goulding, the present General Manager of NTC, the Operating consortium.

Right : The test run is about to cross Talbot Street, heading south. The vertical profile of the road crossing the tramway was caused some design problems and Talbot Street had to be lowered to tie in with the tracks.

Lower right ; The first tests were conducted in the early hours of Sunday mornings, when otherwise busy streets like Cheapside were deserted.

Below : The steep rise of Waverley Street can be seen, as 208 breasts the summit. The length of the vehicle is 33m, which gives an appreciation of the tight radius of the vertical curve that it sits on.

Top Left : The curve from Victoria Street to Fletcher Gate is the tightest on the route, and is coupled with a twist in the vertical geometry, as the line passes the summit. During construction, the rails twisted out of position in the vertical plane, requiring renewal of a section of the rails. The effect that the twisting geometry on the articulation of the trams was the subject of much interest during testing, and an Inspector hrom Her Majesty's Railway Inspectorate watches as 208 carefully heads round the curve.

Bottom Left : A view taken through the window on the return trip shows just how tight the horizontal radius is at this location. It was necessary to reconstruct adjacent footways as part of the tram works, because the surface levels needed to change considerably, in order to accommodate the rails.

Bottom : Running on to the new viaduct at Middle Hill, 208 is subjected to clearance tests. The tram design incorporates a very long overhang at the front. As the tram travels over track that incorporates a vertical curve, the distance between the underside of the nose, and the rails varies. The HMRI lay out stringent criteria regarding the maximum allowable clearance. This is to ensure that the risks of anyone becoming trapped beneath, or run over by a tram is minimised. The steps beneath the doors of the tram had yet to be fitted when this test took place.

A Brief Tour of Wilkinson Street Depot

Right : Tram No 201 receives attention to its front end, after a minor collision with a HGV. The catwalk permits access to the roof mounted electrical equipment.

Lower right ; The wheel turning lathe allows tyres to be reprofiled, without removal of the wheelsets from the trams. An electrically powered shunter positions the trams on the lathe, and moves trams on the section of line beyond that has no overhead.

Below : A general view inside the depot. New tyres are seen in the foreground. These will be fitted to a life expired wheelsets when reprofiling is no longer practical.

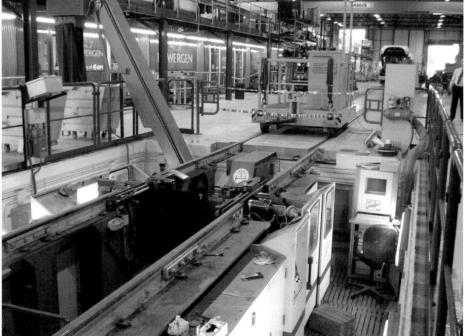

Top : The operating panel of a modern tram is a long way displaced from the simple controls of its Victorian and Edwardian counterparts. David Allen of Booklaw Publications tries out the drivers seat of Tram No 215 in Wilkinson Street Depot.

Bottom : A traction bogie is seen stripped down, part way through a major overhaul.

Top : The computer workstation that controls the wheel turning lathe is situated in a pit adjacent to the lathe. The vehicle tyres are just behind the operators head.

Bottom : A Mercedes 'Unimog' is kept at Wilkinson Street Depot. Its road-rail capabilities make it ideally suited to the task of recovery vehicle, should a tram fail.

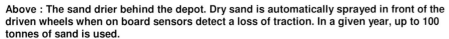

Above : The sand drier behind the depot. Dry sand is automatically sprayed in front of the driven wheels when on board sensors detect a loss of traction. In a given year, up to 100 tonnes of sand is used.

Top Right : The Control Room at Wilkinson Street. Banks of screens cycle round the 80 CCTV cameras that monitor the system.

Bottom Right. Sections of the line are displayed on a series of monitors. These display the locations of the trams, the signals and the points. The Duty Operations Manager communicates to the Drivers by radio.

Appendices:

Appendix 1

Boots Pure Drug Company Rail Traffic from Beeston Factory

The recollections of David Stones, son of Harold Stones,
Boots Despatch Manager in the 1940s & 1950s.

These recollections date from about 1946 when I commenced "collecting engine numbers" as the activity was then called. The nearest railway point to my home was ten to fifteen minutes walk away at Beeston South – as the signal box was called, but the place was known locally as Boots Bridge, being the place where the road into Boots Factory crossed the railway by a bridge. From this vantage point the western end of Beeston Sidings came up to the bridge with four tracks continuing westwards towards Beeston Station. Steps down the eastern side of the bridge led to several cottages at rail level, separated from the railway by a cart track.

The rail access to the Boots railway system was from a trailing junction on the western side of the bridge on the slow line to Beeston.

Up to the mid 1950's at least two trains per day left Boots, each with about a dozen vans and wagons as a minimum. After the mid 1950's this output began to decline as will be explained later. Motive power on these workings in the late 1940's and early 1950's was usually ex LTSR 4-4-2 tank locomotives of the earlier design (LMS numbers 2093-2109) later BR 41910-41926 of which Nottingham Shed had several (2099, 2105 & 2107/8/9 come to mind, plus others. These locos were known to local railwaymen as "Crooners". At times 4F 0-6-0s, 3F 0-6-0Ts (Jinties), 2F 0-6-0s or even occasionally an ex Midland 2P 4-4-0 could be seen bringing loaded vans and wagons out of the factory, then propelling them back into the sidings to be sorted and distributed to their destinations. With the withdrawal of the "Crooners", the other loco classes mentioned became more regular on these shunts. By the early 1960's almost any type of loco still on the Nottingham Shed (16A) allocation might be used, even class 4P 2-6-4 tanks and a BR Standard 3 2-6-0 on one occasion, not long before Boots ceased to transport by rail altogether from the mid 1960's.

My father was manager of the Despatch Department at Boots and as such had the responsibility of ensuring urgently needed Boots products were sent out to the military during the War, as well as supplying Boots own shops' requirements nationwide. I clearly remember him not arriving home most evenings until late, such was the demand for medical products/drugs etc. Of course at that time most industries worked Saturday mornings too. Boots own lorries and vans distributed products to their local branches – probably the

Midlands generally – otherwise the railway transported most of the company output to more distant destinations nationally.

By the mid 1950's road transport was in the ascendant and gradually carried an increasing share of the Boots output. In 1955 the locomotive footplatemens' strike meant that the Boots Company had to urgently look elsewhere for sources of transportation and had no alternative but to engage local road hauliers to move their products over much of the country. As these hauliers were virtually able to guarantee reliable or next day delivery – which the railways increasingly could not – the railway lost the work. Father had several urgent meetings with the local railway management who were apparently astounded by Boots refusal to return to the railway to the same extent as previously once the strike was over. Consequently where there had been at least two or three trains daily – one at about late morning, another at late afternoon, and if my memory is correct, possibly a third train in the evening, the number was reduced to about one per day. Here I am relying on memories from train spotting days and long summer evenings. As we all know, memories are not always reliable.

I took the accompanying photograph in March 1959. It shows ex-LMS 4F 0-6-0 44132 of Nottingham Shed reversing into the sidings at Beeston South with the daily train of loaded vans from Boots sidings.

Ex LT&SR 'Crooner' (Class 2P) No 41925 is seen shortly after Nationalisation, standing outside Nottingham Shed (just visible behind). This engine still carries 'LMS' on its tank side, and was one of several of the class used for local trip working to amongst other locations, Boots.

David Stones Collection

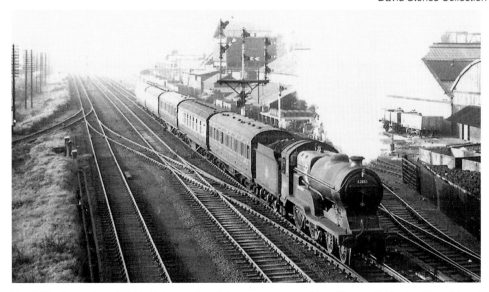

Ex GCR Class D11 62663 'Prince Albert' is seen approaching 'Boots Bridge' with a Lincoln bound train, some time between 1953 and 1957, when the D11s were allocated to Lincoln. The Boots factory connection is seen to the left. Sadly the photographer's details are not known.

David Stones Collection

Appendix 2

Addendum and corrections to Volumes 1 & 2.

Volume One

Page 3 : The network diagram showing the area around Nottingham contains an error at Bottesford West Junction on the Grantham Line, there being no north to east chord.

Page 5 : The caption relating to the Midland Compound contains a typographical error. The class were introduced in 1902, rather than 1920.

Page 8 : The football special photographed by Tony Hill at Midland Station in 1959 was the train conveying the Forest team to the FA Cup Final against Luton Town. Forest won 2-1.

Page 9 : The D11 photographed at the head of the Lincoln Mail (62670) would have been shedded at Lincoln, rather than Darnall. Lincoln (40A) had five of these locomotives at various stages between 1953 and 1957, and 62670 was allocated there from 6/5/56 to 24/3/57. The service was dieselised in 1958 and Volume 2 includes a reproduction of a contemporary publicity leaflet for the replacement service.

Page 13 : The DMU passing Carrington Street goods depot is a Class 114 and not a Class 107 as described in the caption.

Page 15 : The Class 3MT photographed from London Road bridge is more likely to be engaged in empty stock movement rather than heading a passenger service, since it is not occupying the Lincoln road.

Page 23 : The GNR goods sheds between London Road and Manvers Street were sadly still awaiting rescue in early 2009, a victim of a wider economic downturn. The anticipated development that would have seen them restored has been deferred until the market for city centre apartments picks up.

Page 61 : The story related by the author, of the RCTS working on the Nottingham Suburban Railway, stimulated considerable interest. It is fair to say that evidence supporting suggestions that the Railtour was banked by a second locomotive on balance looks pretty shaky, despite coming from one of the footplate crew of the C12 that worked the train. It has been confirmed by one of the original organisers of the trip that the RCTS were only billed for the costs of one locomotive. Additionally, if a second locomotive had been unofficially present, it certainly wasn't positioned in Sneinton Tunnel. A published photograph of the railtour shows the empty bore of the tunnel in the distance. Similarly it would have been seen if it was positioned on the headshunt in Thorneywood Tunnel.

In fairness, the account in Volume 1 was qualified as being possibly just a tall tale from an old railwayman. Of course the spurious engine could have always been hidden in the brickworks tunnel.....

Page 75 : Reference to Langwith Jn on the B1 caption is a typographical error. The locomotive in question was allocated to 40E, but by 1959, this was Colwick's designation, having changed from 38A the previous year.

Page 90 : The underslung bracket signal at the south end of Bridge 289 controlled the Up Main, rather than the Up Goods, as noted in the caption. The unusual configuration of this signal was owed to visibility restrictions imposed by cross bracing on the top of the bridge trusses.

Page 99 : The last spans of the GNR viaduct leading to Weekday Cross Junction were granted a temporary reprieve, and avoided demolition in 2007. Delays in the development of the neighbouring shopping centre mean that the remaining arches will probably remain extant until 2010.

Volume Two

Page 7 : The Johnson tank was actually photographed through Lenton South Box window, the door being at the opposite end of the box.

Page 13 : The Midland Railway freight working thought to be passing through Long Eaton is actually another location. Given its source, it is likely to be somewhere between Nottingham and Derby, but neither the author, nor any of his associates have been able to pin this one down.

Page 16 : Bridge 15 on the Midland's Basford to Bennerley line is unlikely to survive for much longer, and is under threat from the proposed widening of the adjacent motorway.

Page 19 : The signalling at Pinxton was modernised shortly after Volume 2 was published. The signal box was removed, but happily found a home at Barrow Hill Shed, where it has already been re-erected.

Page 31 : The traditional mechanical signalling installations on the Midland line to Lincoln are expected to be replaced by 2012 under the East Midlands Re-signalling project, and the last semaphore signals in the area will disappear.

Page 59 : Dates on captions relating to Ronald Askew's fine pictures of the Annesley Dido are, it seems, inconsistent with allocation records for C12s at Annesley Shed. Sadly the photographer is no longer with us to confirm the dates, but this doesn't diminish these fascinating views of a most unusual working.

Pages 78 & 82 : References to Class 107 DMUs should be Class 114. These were stabled at Lincoln and Derby (Etches Park). The author has little excuse for this recurring mistake since most of the locally stabled 114 units are underlined in his 1980 Ian Allan Locoshed book!

Page 79: The locomotive accompanying the GNR J4 in the photograph near Radcliffe on Trent is not in fact a J3, but a later class J6.

The Author is indebted to a number of correspondents for providing many of the foregoing corrections. It is inevitable that a work of this magnitude will contain some discrepancies, despite extensive proof reading. This is owed to the diverse origins of the source material, the specialist nature of certain information, and the sheer amount that needs to be checked.

Hopefully Volume 3 will have fared slightly better in this respect!

Appendix 3

BR Work Study Dept : Ruddington October 1968

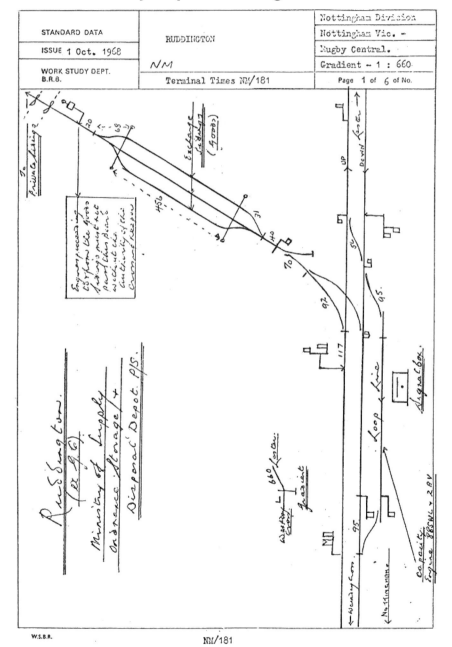

By October 1968, the Great Central London Extension had shrunk to a few isolated sections of line serving industrial concerns. The longest section to retain any form of use after general closure was between Bagthorpe Junction at Basford, and Rugby. When this Work Study was carried out, trains north of Weekday Cross had finished by 5 months, passenger services to Rugby had gone, and the only operational part of the northern section remaining ran from Weekday Cross to Hotchley Hill.

This document records the layout at Ruddington, how trains were shunted into the MoS depot and what type of stock and motive power was typically in use.

OPERATIONS.

1. Up train terminates and forms Down starting train when

    i. run round facilities exist in Exchange Sidings.
    ii. no run round facilities are available in Exchange Sidings.

2. Up train calls to detach when

    i. run round facilities exist in Exchange Sidings.
    ii. no run round facilities are available in Exchange Sidings.

3. Up train terminates in Down Loop.

4. Up train attaches in Down Loop.

5. Down train calls to attach.

6. E.&.2B.V. arrive to form Down starting train.

7. E.&.2 B.V. calls to position wagons from Down Loop in M.O.S. Sidings, depart E.&.2 B.V. or form Down starting train.

SEQUENCE OF MOVEMENTS.

1 i. Train standing on Up Line at director signal to M.O.S. Siding, draws forward into Exchange Sidings. Guard detaches leading B.V., E.&.B.V. run forward and set back to rear of outwards wagons. Engine detached, runs round on third siding, detaches B.V. from rear of inwards wagons and attaches to front of outwards wagons. Guard examines train, confers with driver and joins rear B.V. Train draws forward to outlet signal ready to depart.

ii. If run round facilities are not available in Exchange Sidings, train draws forward along Up Line and sets back to Loop Line, engine runs round via Down Line, re-attaches and propels train through crossover to Up Line and draws along Up Line behind signal controlling access to Exchange Sidings.

Train sets back to Exchange Sidings, detaches rear B.V. to front of outwards wagons and shunts inwards wagons to Siding. Engine detaches and moves to attach to outwards wagons, draws forward and sets back to attach B.V. off inward wagons. Train examined, Guard in rear B.V., train stands partly on Down Line ready to depart.

SEQUENCE OF MOVEMENTS (Cont/...)

2 i. Train standing on Up Line at director signal to M.O.S. Siding. Guard walks, detaches behind inwards wagons and ascends engine. Engine and wagons draw forward to Exchange Sidings. Wagons detached, E.&.B.V. draw forward and runs back through adjacent Siding to rear portion of train. Guard attaches and joins rear B.V. Train standing at Home Signal ready to depart.

ii. If run round facilities are not available in Exchange Sidings, Guard detaches inwards wagons, engine and wagons draw forward and set back to Down Loop for engine to run round and return to Up Line behind director signal.

B.V., Engine and wagons set back to Exchange Sidings, wagons detached, engine propels B.V. to rear portion of train and attaches. Guard joins rear B.V., train standing at Home Signal ready to depart.

3. Train standing on Up Line at Home Signal draws forward to detach rear B.V. inside Home Signal. Engine, front B.V., and wagons draw forward and set back to Down Loop. Wagons detached, E.&.B.V. return to Up Line and set back to second B.V. to attach. E.&.2 B.V. stand at Home Signal ready to depart.

4. Train standing on Up Line at Home Signal, engine and front B.V. detached, draw forward and set back to Down Loop. Wagons examined and attached, engine and wagons draw forward to Up Line and set back to rear portion and attach. Guard joins rear B.V., train ready to depart.

5. Train standing on Down Line at Home Signal draws forward, engine and front B.V. detached draw clear of access points and set back to Exchange Sidings. Wagons examined and attached, engine and wagons draw forward to Down Line, set back to rear portion and attach. Guard joins rear B.V., train ready to depart.

6. Engine with 2 B.V. propelled standing on Up Line at Home Signal, propels and detaches leading B.V. on suitable road in Exchange Sidings. E.&.B.V. move onto outwards wagons, wagons examined and attached. Engine and wagons draw forward and set back to rear B.V. and attach. Guard in B.V. train standing partly on Down Line ready to depart.

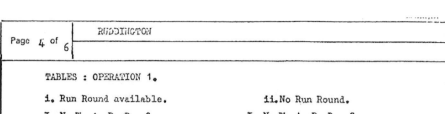

TABLES : OPERATION 1.

i. Run Round available.

OUTWARDS \ INWARDS	30	40	50
30	26	27	28
40	32	32	33
50	34	35	36

ii. No Run Round.

OUTWARDS \ INWARDS	30	40	50
30	19	20	21
40	22	23	24
50	26	26	27

RUN ROUND ALLOWANCE - ONLY APPLICABLE WHEN
NO RUN ROUND FACILITY IS AVAILABLE - 19 Minutes.

TIMES START   Train standing on Up Line at signal controlling entrance to M.O.S. Sidings, train ready to enter Sidings.

TIMES FINISH i. Train standing at outlet signal controlling exit from M.O.S. Sidings.

          ii. Train standing partly on Down Line with rear B.V. in Exchange Sidings.

OPERATION 2.

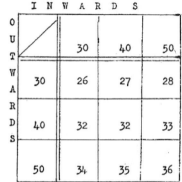

i. Run Round available

	INWARDS
	30
LE	20

ii. No Run Round available.

	INWARDS
	30
	14

RUN ROUND ALLOWANCE - ONLY APPLICABLE WHEN
NO RUN ROUND FACILITY IS AVAILABLE - 14 Minutes.

TIMES START   Train or engine and wagons standing on Up Line at signal controlling entrance to M.O.S. Sidings, ready to enter Sidings.

TIMES FINISH Train standing on Up Line at Home Signal ready to depart.

NM/181

OPERATION 3.

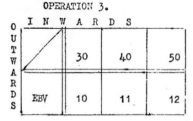

OUTWARDS \ INWARDS	30	40	50
EBV	10	11	12

TIMES START AND FINISH   Train or E.& 2 B.V. standing on Up Line at Home Signal.

OPERATION 4.

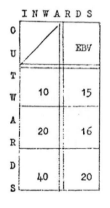

INWARDS	
	EBV
10	15
20	16
40	20

TIMES START AND FINISH.   Train standing on Up Line at Home Signal.

OPERATION 5.

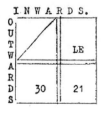

INWARDS	
	LE
30	21

TIMES START   Train standing on Down Line at Home Signal.

TIMES FINISH Train standing on Down Line adjacent to Signal Box ready to depart.

NM/181

OPERATION 6.

INWARDS

O U T W A R D S		EBV
	30	17
	40	20
	50	22

TIMES START — E.&.2 B.V. standing on Up Line at Home Signal.

TIMES FINISH — Train standing partly on Down Line with rear B.V. in Exchange Sidings.

OPERATION 7.

INWARDS

SHUNT ALLOWANCE — Run round wagons in Down Loop and position wagons in Exchange Sidings :-

Wagons on Down Loop	30	40	50
Minutes	18	19	21

O U T W A R D S		EBV
	EBV	1
	30	14
	40	17
	50	20

TIMES START — E.&.2 B.V. standing on Up Line at Home Signal.

TIMES FINISH — E.&.2 B.V. standing in M.O.S. Siding at outlet signal or train standing partly on Down Line with rear B.V. in Exchange Sidings.

LOCO.	Diesel Types 1 or 2.
M.P.D.	Nottingham and Colwick
TRAIN	Class 8 Unfitted
LOAD LIMIT	Type 2 60 B.W.U. Down
	" 71 B.W.U. Up
	Type 4 88 " Down
	" 104 " Up
LENGTH LIMIT	80
TRAFFIC	Various, loaded and empty.
PACE OF MOVEMENT.	Unrestricted, Restricted.
SPECIAL CONDITIONS.	B.V. provided at each end of train to facilitate run rounds en route from Colwick or Nottingham.

Bibliography

Whilst numerous information sources were used during the research of this book, specific reference was made to the following publications and documents. Every effort has been made to ensure that information is reproduced correctly, however any errors or omissions are wholly the Author's responsibility.

NET Highway Maintenance Manual
Nottingham City Council
H J Reed

Great Northern Railway Act 1880
Indicative Alignment Plans
(Reproduced from Ordnance Survey Mapping)

The Great Northern Railway
O S Nock

The Great Northern and London & North Western Joint Railway
D L Franks

The Locomotive Magazine
February 1912

The Great Northern Railway in the East Midlands Vols 1-4
A Henshaw

Tracks to the Cities
The Permanent Way Institution
David L Bateman

An Illustrated History of Great Northern Railway Signalling
M A Vanns

The Development of Nottingham's Railways
J P Wilson

The Railways of Newark on Trent
M A Vanns

The Great Central Then & Now
M Hawkins

Industrial Steam Locomotives of Central England
Warwickshire Railway Society (1966)

Industrial Locomotives of the East Midlands
The Birmingham Locomotive Club (1947)

Ordnance Survey County Series 1:2500 mapping.

Acknowledgements

The author is indebted to the following individuals, organisations and companies for their assistance during the writing of this book. Their contributions, through allowing access to private collections and unpublished reference material, and arranging permission to visit restricted sites has made completion of the work possible, and broadened the author's knowledge along the way.

David Allen
Ian Askew
John Bull
Rob Hancock
Tom Hawkins
Graham Jelly
Clive Pennington
David Stones
Peter Wilson
Anne Winfindale / DTZ Security
Building Design Partnership Ltd
Network Rail
Nottingham City Council
Nottingham City Transport
Nottingham Magistrates Court
Nottingham Model Railway Society
Nottingham Tram Consortium
Nottingham Transport Heritage Centre